# Just an Animal

PET CHAPLAIN LEARNING SERIES • VOLUME 3

# Just an Animal

## Reflections on the Human-Animal Bond and Western Culture

Rob Gierka, EdD
Karen Duke

Published by Pet Chapel® Press (petchapel.com/press). Pet Chaplain® and Pet Chapel® are registered trademarks.



Book design by Karen Duke.

Paperback ISBN 978-1-969169-07-6
Kindle ISBN 978-1-969169-08-3
Ebook ISBN 978-978-1-969169-06-9

First edition 2026.

# Pet Chaplain® Learning Series

### VOLUME 1

## Heart Animals
Sacred Stories About Pets Who Change Our Lives

### VOLUME 2

## Always in My Heart
Coping Creatively with Pet Loss

### VOLUME 3

## Just an Animal
Reflections on the Human-Animal Bond and Western Culture

### VOLUME 4

## Veterinary Chaplaincy
Interfaith Spiritual Care for Pet Loss

Visit petchaplain.com to learn more about the series
and other resources available from Pet Chaplain.

This book is dedicated to all the amazing animals
of this world. Our lives are infinitely richer
because of your presence.

People who say things like, "Oh, it was just a dog or a cat" have never had that bond with an animal. It's the same as somebody never knowing love and that's a terrible thing.

— Lillian

Reflecting on her sixteen-year relationship
with a giant Maine coon named Freddie

# Contents

# A Note from the Authors

Welcome to the Pet Chaplain Learning Series! I'm Rob Gierka, founder and president of Pet Chaplain, and I'll be your guide for this unique learning experience. In this introductory note, I'll provide some essential information about the series, including an overview of its goals and recommendations for engaging with the books.

This book is the third volume in a four-book set that explores pet keeping and loss in contemporary Western society. If you're passionate about pets, concerned with the well-being of all animals, or simply curious about the human-animal bond, you'll learn a great deal about this remarkable social and cultural phenomenon with this series. If you've recently lost a pet and are struggling with grief—or if you're thinking about a pet lost years before—you'll find the support you need within one or all of the first three books in the series. These volumes examine pet keeping and loss from different angles so you can explore your experience holistically. The fourth book in the series builds on the content of the first three books with a focus on interfaith spiritual care for pet loss, providing an invaluable resource for caregiving professionals and others interested in this new field of spiritual care.

The series addresses four primary questions: Why are our animal companions so important to us? How do we navigate the deep sorrow we experience as we rebuild our lives without their physical presence? How do our social interactions impact our journey of grief when we lose our pets? And how can we best help each other find lasting peace and a renewed sense of purpose? The series explores these queries through a combination of scholarship and storytelling that vividly capture the lived reality of pet keeping and loss in the modern West.

Regarding scholarship, the series takes a broad, interdisciplinary approach. It draws on many academic disciplines, including human-animal studies, clinical psychology, existential psychology, death studies, philosophy, sociology, anthropology, religious studies, history, and neuroscience. This holistic approach is increasingly rare in today's siloed academic world, where most scholars focus solely on their area of expertise. Yet life is not easily divided into neat categories, and I've taken considerable care to synthesize the research cited in the series into a holistic perspective on our complex, continually evolving relationship with the greater-than-human world. Geographically, however, I've had to limit my research because it was impractical to incorporate scholarship for locations outside the West. Most of the research about pet keeping and loss, the human experience of grief, and other topics covered in the series is based on studies conducted in the US and, to a lesser extent, Canada, Australia, and Western Europe.

To balance out all this scholarship, the series includes an abundance of pet stories. These narratives are important not only because people love to read stories but because stories are critical to a good education. There's an old proverb that says: "Tell me the facts, and I'll learn. Tell me the truth, and I'll believe. But tell me a story, and it will live in my heart forever." When you've read everything I have to say about pet keeping and loss, I expect it's the stories you'll remember best.

Many voices make an appearance in the series. I tell my own stories about pets I've loved and lost and the pivotal experiences that have shaped my interest in this new field of spiritual care. You'll read the stories of pet keepers who attended my pet loss support group over the last two decades. You'll gain insight into the veterinary world as I reflect on my service as the on-call chaplain at a large veterinary teaching hospital. You'll read the stories and reflections of people who participated in an online course in veterinary chaplaincy that my co-author Karen Duke and I developed and taught for five years. Finally, you'll discover the amazing insights offered by a small group of aspiring veterinary technologists ("vet techs") who I interviewed for my doctoral research study of the human-animal bond and bereavement.

The four volumes that comprise the series are not textbooks per se, or at least not the kind of textbook you may have read before. As an educational program, the series is modeled on the self-paced courses offered by the Great Books Foundation, a nonprofit organization that promotes lifelong learning through reading and discussion of literature, philosophy, poetry, and other compelling texts. For fourteen years, I participated in a Great Books discussion group with a small group of well-read and highly accomplished octogenarians. It was one of the best learning experiences of my life, and I've long wanted to create a rich, transformative learning experience for others.

One of the series' greatest strengths—and the quality that sets it apart from other books about pet keeping and loss—is its wealth of learning resources. The first three books in the series include thought-provoking questions that encourage critical engagement with many concepts related to pet keeping and loss, giving you the opportunity to articulate your beliefs on a variety of animal-related topics. There are no "right" answers to these questions. Rather, their goal is to promote critical thinking, exploration, analysis, and the clear articulation of your personal perspective on the diverse topics explored in the series. The more time and effort you put into this work, the more you'll learn about yourself and your perspective about animals, death, grief, spirituality, and other topics explored in the series.

You'll also be invited to create what I call a "sacred story"—or, more accurately, a series of stories—about your life as an animal lover, pet keeper, animal advocate, environmentalist, or however you might describe yourself. A sacred story aims to answer some simple but challenging questions: What is your authentic identity as a human being amid all the diverse life-forms on this incredible planet? How have your personal interactions with animals and the natural world shaped your identity? And how can you lead a life in relationship with animals and the natural world that is spiritually directed and in keeping with your values? If such questions are important to you, then you're in the right place.

This kind of contemplative practice is essential in this age of rapid technological, cultural, and environmental change. Amid these vast shifts, many people are adopting new perspectives about the greater-than-human world. The spiritual landscape in the modern West is also changing. Among those who participate in a mainstream faith community, many approach their spiritual lives from a position of searching and questioning. Many people have left mainstream faith communities and are creating spiritual amalgamations that blend scientific understandings of the cosmos with traditional faith traditions and ancient spiritual practices. Still others contemplate the world through a values-based or humanist lens. Wherever you place yourself in this evolving spiritual landscape, the learning series will help you better understand the origins of your values and beliefs about animals and spirituality.

You can read these books from personal interest or to support your healing journey, whether you're anticipating the imminent loss of a pet, actively grieving for a pet, or thinking about a pet lost years ago. The series' learning resources also make it a great fit for book study groups, and I encourage you to seek out others with whom you can share this journey of learning, healing, and spiritual growth. Your group might include your family and friends, coworkers, fellow church members in your place of worship, animal lovers you know through social media groups, or even people you meet at the dog park. Sharing your stories about animals and receiving others' stories with compassion will broaden your perspective on the human-animal bond and expand your ability to appreciate the diverse ways people think about and interact with animals.

The learning series is the culmination of thirty years of study, personal contemplation, spiritual care practice, and creative collaboration with pet keepers, animal advocates, environmentalists, and spiritual seekers. As noted earlier, I'll serve as your narrator and guide throughout the series, but it's important to note that my coauthor Karen has supported me throughout the development process. A talented writer and artist, Karen has helped me condense, organize, and synthesize years of practical insights and scholarship, and she's also contributed her own research to the wealth of scholarship cited in these books. Karen was also the lead writer for the series, so her voice is on every page, even when I appear to be doing all the talking.

Thank you for your interest in the Pet Chaplain Learning Series. Karen and I are delighted and humbled by the opportunity to share all we've learned with you. We hope you enjoy this learning experience and that, wherever your path may take you, you'll have a richer understanding of why animals are such an important part of our lives.

With gratitude—
Rob Gierka, EdD, and Karen Duke

# Introduction

One of my favorite scenes in the classic film *The Wizard of Oz*, is when Dorothy, her three new friends, and her dog Toto visit the great wizard in the Emerald City. Dorothy and Toto are trying to find their way back to their home in Kansas, the Scarecrow is seeking a brain, the Tin Man a heart, and the Cowardly Lion courage. But the wizard is not the wise, kindly man they expected. Instead, they meet a larger-than-life, godlike figure on a giant screen who insists that, if they want his help, they must bring him the broomstick of the Wicked Witch of the West.

The group set off on a long and difficult journey in which the travelers negotiate their greatest fears. After much travail, they finally capture the witch's broomstick and return to the Emerald City for their hard-earned reward. But the wizard inexplicably rescinds his promise to grant them their wishes. It's only when little Toto pulls back the curtain that the wizard is hiding behind that we learn that the "great and powerful Oz" is just an ordinary guy who, like Dorothy and her friends, is also lost.

This scene holds some important lessons. We learn that human beings are easily frightened, and because of our fears, we often mask our true identities. Animals, however, rarely exhibit such duplicity. They are who they are, and, like muses who call forth our truest selves, they reveal who we are as well. Toto's revelation about the wizard's true identity paved the way for the four travelers to discover their authentic selves—to find the home, the brain, the heart, and the courage they already possessed but failed to see.

In this book, I've attempted to follow Toto's lead and pull back the curtain on the perplexing and contradictory ways we think about and interact with the animals in our midst. If language offers a window into a society's values, then statements like "just an animal" tell you a lot about our prevailing beliefs about animals. The word *just* is semantically loaded. It implies that animals' lives don't really matter and that if you grieve for the loss of an animal, then surely something must be wrong with you. This book flips this strange bit of logic on its head by celebrating the unique ways animals enrich our lives. When we consider all we lose when a beloved pet dies or is otherwise lost, our grief should not be reduced to an overreaction to a minor loss but respected as a reasonable response to the loss of an important relationship.

The loss of a human loved one is almost always honored in our society according to well-understood norms of mourning. But the loss of a pet can be a lonely journey full of uncertainty. Pet keepers often grieve alone because they worry that others won't understand their feelings, or they fear being judged harshly, especially when their grief is intense. Many also lack access to the familiar and comforting markers of public ritual that we use to honor the passing of a human loved one.

This reality is not entirely a matter of a few insensitive people who don't know how to respond to others' suffering. It is, more accurately, an unavoidable consequence of our culture. The Western world is dominated by a centuries-old paradigm that tells us in countless ways that nonhuman animals are inferior to humans in almost all the measures we claim matter to us, from language and intelligence to emotional complexity and morality. This enduring but inaccurate perspective has cast a shadow on people who love animals and grieve their loss. We live in a society that celebrates pet keeping and in which most households keep pets, yet collectively we do not always treat the animals in our midst with respect and compassion. Our society also has strong and diverse religious traditions but neglects the need for spiritual support when we lose animals who are much-loved members of our families. Such incongruities are symptomatic of a cultural divide between people who love animals, those who view them solely as useful objects, and those who fall somewhere between the two extremes

This book offers a critical perspective on pet keeping in the modern West, situating it within the larger framework of the evolving relationship between humans and animals. In explicating this complex topic, I cast a wide net. You'll learn how philosophers, religious leaders, and scientists have depicted animals through the ages and how these perspectives have changed in recent decades. When you finish this book, you'll better understand why you might sometimes feel isolated in a society where animals are not always valued. If you've ever wished for a simple service or prayer when your animal passed away, or you've hesitated to approach your religious leader for counsel and comfort, or your family, friends, or coworkers have grown impatient with your grief, this book will be an affirming read that reveals the subtle and often hidden reasons why pet loss can be such a lonely, challenging experience.

We'll begin this journey with a critical look at the human-animal bond. My goal in the first three chapters is to deconstruct the bond and offer a frank account of the paradoxes and contradictions that characterize our relationships with animals, including those species commonly kept as pets. We are, after all, one half of the equation in the human-animal bond. If we want to fully appreciate the complexity of our relationship with other animals, including our pets, we must first be honest with ourselves about who we are as a species.

As part of this exploration, I'll discuss the deep-seated psychological phenomenon that compels us to denigrate animals. As you'll see, regarding animals as lesser beings and distancing ourselves from them may be an unavoidable aspect of human nature. It's difficult to acknowledge the indifference and cruelty with which the human animal often treats other living creatures. In researching this book, I sometimes felt embarrassed about my own humanness. Yet we're as capable of compassion as we are of cruelty, and I remain hopeful that our better selves will prevail as the human-animal bond continues to evolve, and we embrace our fellow creatures as fellow travelers in this life rather than seeing them only as our underlings.

This book explores some of the more troubling aspects of pet keeping and loss in the modern West, from the way animals are legally classified as property to the social and religious alienation that is distressingly common in the pet-keeping community. Yet it ultimately has a happy ending—or at least the promise of one—when it comes to animals. Indeed, we're beginning to tell a new story about animals that provides a refreshing alternative to the narrative we've inherited from our forebears. In the book's final chapters, I'll explore how ethicists, theologians, and other animal advocates are challenging the dominant philosophical and religious paradigms that have depicted animals as lesser creatures than humans. We'll also consider new scientific understandings of animal cognition and emotions that are changing the conversation about animals among academic researchers and, increasingly, among everyday people.

People who keep pets are also telling inspiring stories about their animal friends. We've learned firsthand that our animal companions are unique individuals with superior senses, exquisite sensitivity to body language and mood, and great emotional intelligence. Our pets bring pure, uncomplicated affection to our lives and a comforting connection that transcends the need for words. They also possess many fine qualities that we sometimes struggle to find in human relationships, such as the ability to love without judgment. One of the vet techs I interviewed for my doctoral research project, a man named Frank, observed that once you've enjoyed unconditional love with an animal, you never forget it. I believe Frank is right. A faithful, caring relationship with an animal can be transformative. I've met many people who claim to have never had much interest in animals until one day a pet came into their life, they fell in love, and their perspective changed from indifference to profound love and respect. Today, animal advocacy is growing rapidly, particularly among young people, and this shift toward a more egalitarian and respectful relationship with animals and nature is fueled, in part, by the powerful bonds we enjoy with our pets.

I believe we're in the midst of a massive paradigm shift in our collective relationship with the greater-than-human world. The term *paradigm shift* was introduced by American physicist and philosopher of science Thomas Kuhn in his 1962 groundbreaking book, *The Structure of Scientific Revolutions*.[1] Kuhn argued that scientific paradigms remain constant until we become aware of some new phenomenon that doesn't fit the current paradigm. Eventually, society adopts a new paradigm, though this process generally takes a very long time, and changes occur in fits and starts. Moreover, paradigm shifts are often accompanied by great controversy and even acrimony, as scientists invested in old paradigms refuse to accept the work of those who challenge conventional thinking. Although Kuhn's analysis was focused specifically on the world of science, his observations hold true for other aspects of our lives, including our relationships with animals and our spiritual and religious beliefs.

In writing this book, I've sought primarily to inform and inspire you. Yet I also want to encourage you to reflect critically on the messages we receive about animals in our society. Culture is like water we're all swimming in. It's all around us, even inside us, yet most of us are not fully aware of its existence. In a commencement address at Kenyon College in 2005, American comedian and writer David Foster told an insightful joke about the difficulty of seeing our own culture for what it is: "There are these two young fish swimming along, and they happen to meet an older fish swimming the other way, who nods at them and says, 'Morning, boys. How's the water?' And the two young fish swim on for a bit, and then eventually one of them looks over at the other and goes 'What the hell is water?'"[2]

My interest in cultural critique was inspired by the great Brazilian educator and philosopher Paulo Freire, who coined the term *conscientization* to describe a change in our conscious awareness of systematic oppression in society. In *Pedagogy of the Oppressed*, Freire asserted that to make positive changes in the world, we must first gain a critical awareness of our social reality.[3] We must acknowledge—honestly and fearlessly—the way in which our society privileges some and disenfranchises others, and act to rectify these shortcomings. Freire died in 1997, but his work continues to have a profound impact on educators and social activists.

In the spirit of *conscientization*, this book documents the disenfranchisement of animals in Western society and reveals how it impacts the people who love them. It will help you understand how the disenfranchisement of animals has impacted your own life. To this end, I encourage you to engage with the discussion questions presented throughout the book. In addition, the final chapter includes the third round of the sacred story project that was presented in the first and second books of the Pet Chaplain Learning Series. The sacred story project is intended to help you understand the connections between your experiences with animals, your core values and beliefs, and your guiding purpose in life. The exercise presented here will encourage you to reflect on your social experiences relative to animals, broadening your awareness of the many cultural influences that have shaped your spiritual journey thus far.

For readers interested in the practice of veterinary chaplaincy, this book offers a big-picture perspective of the cultural stage in which our relationships with our animal companions play out. The way we think about and interact with animals varies significantly in the West. Understanding these differences and their historical roots will prepare you to help grieving pet keepers navigate the social and religious disenfranchisement that is common in the pet-keeping community.

The unvarnished perspective of our society's paradoxical relationship with animals that I offer in these pages may be especially meaningful to people who work with animals. Veterinary professionals and animal rescue workers regularly encounter people who treat animals like disposable objects, so they know first hand how animals and people alike suffer because of our society's habitual denigration of animals. The experience is much the same for people who grieve the loss of wild animals and natural, untouched places. Students in my veterinary chaplaincy course often expressed sadness, anger, and even despair about the ongoing loss of wild animals. For some, it was the first time they'd ever fully revealed the depth of their despair because it can be difficult to find social settings where it's safe to share such sentiments.

No matter who you are or why you've picked up this book, I encourage you to respond honestly to the ideas and information I offer. What resonates with you, what doesn't, and why? Adults learn differently than young children. As we mature and navigate life's ups and downs, we spiral back and reflect on our past experiences to gain new learning. Every new event or idea we encounter in life is weighed against our existing understanding of the world, sometimes supporting our worldview, sometimes challenging it. You may not agree with everything I say about animals, spirituality, religion, science, and the many other topics explored in these pages. Yet I don't believe in truth with a capital T. In the wise words of historian and philosopher Will Durant, "We are all drops of water trying to analyze the sea."[4] You have your own truth about animals and spirituality, and this book is intended to help you define and express your truth.

# Deconstructing the Human-Animal Bond

## CHAPTER 1

# A Tale of Two Rabbits

I've always adored rabbits, but I never knew much about them until I read the book *Stories Rabbits Tell* by Margo DeMello and Susan B. Davis.[1] DeMello is a cultural anthropologist who has written numerous books about the human-animal bond, and Davis is a journalist and editor. Both are rabbit enthusiasts. When they began researching and writing about the domesticated rabbit, Susan had a pair of indoor rabbits, and Margo was fostering a herd of twenty-two rabbits, who lived comfortably in a spacious indoor rabbit room.

Rabbits are normally shy animals. But according to DeMello and Davis, when these long-eared, short-legged animals are allowed to roam freely in a safe space, they'll "jump, dance, groom, climb, fight, explore, lick, roll on their backs, love, play tag and in general behave in ways no one could imagine by observing them in cages. . . . They can be smart or dull, athletic or lazy, patient or impulsive, affectionate or aloof."[2] People with pet rabbits discover that these fascinating creatures are unique individuals with distinct personalities, just like dogs and cats. They're intelligent, clever, highly emotional, playful, and fun to have around. They're gorgeous, with incredibly soft fur of varying colors, lengths, and patterns. They're easily litter trained. Finally, they're very affectionate, though they prefer to be petted on the floor rather than being held in your lap.

Although they make great pets, rabbits are not the same as our canine and feline friends. This became apparent to me when I saw the movie *Roger & Me* by director Michael Moore. Moore and his film crew were visiting a woman in a neighborhood outside Detroit, Michigan. A hand-painted cardboard sign hanging on the front porch advertised rabbits for sale, either as pets or meat. As the scene unfolded, Moore and his camera crew followed the woman to a large rabbit hutch in her backyard. She removed a large rabbit from the hutch and stroked him as she held him against her chest. Then with quick, practiced movements, she lifted the rabbit up by his hind legs, pulled a knife from her pocket, slit his throat, and pulled off his skin as if she were pulling off a sock.

This horrific scene caused a stir among animal rights activists, who objected to Moore's inclusion of this violent scene in the film. Moore responded by accusing the activists of being more concerned with the rabbit than with the plight of a woman who was struggling to survive in modern-day Detroit.

Such controversy aside, what struck me about the scene was the juxtaposition of the words *pet* and *meat* to describe the same animal. Regarding animals in different ways—even the same animal—is common in all cultures. Humans have simultaneously loved animals, reviled them, worshipped them, abused them, revered them, and sacrificed them. Such contradictions existed in ancient civilizations and persist to this day.

Humans are complex and sometimes perplexing creatures. We have an amazing ability to live with paradox and tolerate the dissonance that arises because of these contradictions. Nowhere is our proclivity for contradictory thinking more apparent than in our relationships with animals. As a society, we welcome dogs and cats into our homes as pets while these same animals are used as test subjects in laboratories. We claim to love wild animals yet fail to appreciate the connection between the loss of natural habitat and the growth of large-scale industrial agriculture that serves the needs of a growing human population. Many of us feel uncomfortable when we consider the plight of animals in the modern world. But we're inclined to quickly push aside such unpleasant realities, or we justify them with the rationale that animals must be sacrificed for the sake of human health and well-being. Of course, the worst aspects of our treatment of animals are concerned are carefully hidden from public view, making it easy for us to carry on with our lives without really looking too hard at our less-than-stellar behavior. Yet as I've said, it's also true that millions of people despair over animal suffering but feel powerless to change the status quo.

Whatever your personal experience might be, the truth is unavoidable. In the modern West, the way we think about and interact with the animals in our midst depends a lot on what kind of animal they are. Dogs and cats are pets. Cows, pigs, and chickens are food animals. But rabbits fall somewhere in between. They're given a dual purpose—pets for some, food for others—complicating the logic we use for classifying animals. Rabbits have not crossed the cultural boundary that makes eating cats, dogs, and horses taboo. Undoubtedly, rabbit enthusiasts like DeMello and Davis are horrified that some of their neighbors eat the animals they adore.

Grasping the incredibly diverse ways we interact with animals is a monumental task. Different people think differently about different animals depending on where they live, what they do for a living, their daily interactions with animals, whether they keep pets, their family history of pet keeping, their culture and subculture, the media they consume, their age and gender, and so on. In recent decades, an increasing number of scientists and researchers have dedicated their careers to studying the evolving relationship between humans and animals. So what do these scholars have to say about the diversity of human-animal relationships in Western society? And what can we learn about human beings from this research?

## From Pets to Pests

Beginning in the 1970s, a new field of study known as anthrozoology or Human-Animal Studies (HAS) emerged in the academic world. HAS is an interdisciplinary field that focuses on the intersection between people and animals. Pet keeping is a top concern in this young academic field. Most HAS research addresses the psychological and biological underpinnings of people's attachments to pets, attitudes toward the use of animals in laboratory experiments, cross-cultural similarities and differences in human-animal relationships, and gender differences in pet keeping.

Among the most interesting outcomes of HAS academic work is the development of elaborate classification systems for animals known as *human-animal bond scales*. One scale offered by veterinarian Alice Villalobos reveals the complexity and diversity in the way we value and treat our fellow creatures. Referred to as the Universal Human-Animal Bond Scale, this schematic is based on a rubric of "attachment, devotion, value, concern, and responsibility."[3] In the list below, animals are divided into categories, with those that are most valued at the top and least valued at the bottom:

1.  A love relationship with two-way interaction between a person and a specific companion animal who is regarded as a best friend or a member of the family. Emotional attachment and reciprocal reliance are readily displayed.

2.  A strong relationship but yields to other responsibilities and priorities.

3.  Successive reliance relationships, such as service animals, K-9 partners, etc.

4.  Ownership for a purpose, such as military, protection, work, transport, etc.

5.  Animals used in racing, hunting, sports, shows, and the circus.

6. Animals raised in a family environment but considered disposable.

7. Casual interactions with therapy, aquarium, zoo, and exhibit animals.

8. Food animals, farmed animals, game reserves, and game animals.

9. Species exploited for sport-fighting and other abusive acts.

10. Laboratory animals used in research and development.

11. Reserve and free-ranging wild animals, wild birds, and aquatic animals.

12. Unwanted animals, including horses, dogs, cats, feral animals, hoarded animals, etc.

13. Invasive species, pests, parasites, vectors of disease, and destructive species that harm people and livestock.

Although Villalobos's scale appears to be comprehensive, it's not truly "universal." There's no mention, for example, of animals who are considered sacred. In India, where Hinduism is widespread, some are considered sacred, including cows and dogs. Another problem with this model is the level of attachment Villalobos assigns to people who engage with animals in "reliance relationships," such as service animals. Research has shown that people with service animals are deeply attached to their animal partners, so I expect the ranking is too low.[4] Despite these limitations, Villalobos's scale provides a helpful summary of the wildly different ways in which Westerners and many other people around the world think about animals.

In terms of companion animals, Villalobos's scale shows that people keep pets for many different reasons, ranging from a "love relationship" at the top of the list to "disposable" animals in the middle of the list. Another scale by veterinarian Michael Fox focuses solely on pets and offers an even more nuanced understanding of person-pet relationships:

1. The actualizing relationship, in which the person's relationship with the animal is fully equal and based on mutual respect.

2. The need-dependency relationship, in which the animal satisfies the individual's need for companionship.

3. The object-oriented relationship, in which the pet is seen as a novelty or a decorative item.

4. The utilitarian relationship, in which the animal is used to provide a specific benefit to people, such as being a guard dog.[5]

As granular as these two scales are, however, they don't fully capture the nuances of many person-pet relationships. For any individual, the lines between the various classifications can be blurry. Dog and cat fanciers who pursue the perfect pedigree for their animal may appear to regard their pets as prized possessions or objects to manipulate and control. Yet their keen interest in shaping their animal to rarefied standards of physical conformation does not preclude feelings of love and admiration for that animal. In addition, many suburban families have formed strong emotional attachments to animals traditionally used as food, such as chickens, a trend that has picked up steam with the increasingly popular practice of keeping a backyard coop for fresh egg production. Similarly, pets may be kept for utilitarian purposes, such as a hunting dog, but the hunter might still regard their dog with considerable affection and a powerful sense of shared purpose, camaraderie, and connection.

These depictions of the human-animal bond may not be entirely accurate, but they do offer great insight into the human animal who created them. To begin with, it's apparent that we humans are strongly inclined to divide and categorize the world around us. This is an immensely useful skill, and it could be argued that it's necessary for our survival. It's certainly in our best interest to know which animals are dangerous and which are not. But it's equally valid to say that viewing animals solely in terms of their usefulness is a narrow way to depict the incredible diversity of life on this planet.

On this point, another observation about these scales is that they're consistently self-serving. In making this point, I have to admit I feel a little chagrined. After all, no one wants to admit that they're selfish. Yet it's undeniable that animals have a certain value because we say they do. This is referred to as an animal's *instrumental value.* In contrast, the phrase *intrinsic value* refers to the belief that a living being is valuable simply by virtue of being alive and having the will to live. Humans are believed to have intrinsic value, while most nonhuman life-forms are categorized according to their instrumental value. Many people who keep pets undoubtedly believe their animal has intrinsic value. Yet Fox's scale of person-pet relationships shows that not everyone who keeps pets shares this perspective.

It's also worth considering the broader implications of our habit of organizing and classifying the natural world. Is it possible we've become so accustomed to the labels we apply to animals that we fail to appreciate the unique qualities of the creatures themselves? Do we see animals solely based on our assumptions about them without truly understanding them as individuals and the vital role they play in the earth's many ecosystems? Indeed, as a species, humans can be remarkably myopic. We see the world narrowly, through the lens of our personal wants and needs. In doing so, we struggle to appreciate the complexity of this world beyond our own immediate concerns. HAS scholar Margo DeMello is one of the rabbit enthusiasts I introduced at the beginning of this chapter. She points out that "being an animal in human society has little to do with biology and almost everything to do with human culture. Animals' physical identity is less important to their status and treatment than their symbolic identification and their social meaning."[6]

In a word, human beings are *anthropocentric,* which is defined as "the belief that all value is human-centered. The interests and perspectives of humanity are privileged, and the value of other species is determined primarily by their utility to human beings."[7] Of course, anthropocentric thinking is more pronounced in some people than others. At an extreme, people who are highly anthropocentric completely dismiss the possibility that animals have any intrinsic value whatsoever. Research supports this conclusion. A British study found that people with strongly anthropocentric beliefs tend to view lower-status animals, such as food animals, less attractive wild animals (e.g., snakes and rats), and pests, as having no moral status whatsoever.[8] People with this mindset believe these animals lack emotions and the advanced cognitive abilities that warrant moral consideration. According to the study authors, people who look at the world this way will overlook any similarities between lower-status animals and human beings, and they're "more inclined to perceive [the] negative or undesirable features of these animals."[9] Similarly, a study of US adults found that "animals perceived as more similar to humans are treated better than those considered less similar. People show greater discomfort when led to believe they are watching the abuse of an animal similar to humans; they recommend significantly more jail time and larger fines for abusers of these animals, and they prefer to save endangered species most similar to humans."[10]

Research also shows that people who are strongly anthropocentric embrace hierarchical thinking to justify maintaining the status quo in which animals are used to serve human needs, regardless of the impact on the animals themselves or the health of planetary ecosystems.[11] Moreover, people with an anthropocentric mindset tend to see *all* living beings in a hierarchical way, including other people. That is, those who regard animals with disdain also view low-status groups of people (e.g., the poor, the disabled) as inherently inferior to higher-status groups (e.g., the wealthy, able-bodied people).[12] In other words, the oppression of socially ostracized groups of all kinds—from low-status animals to low-status people—flows from the same hier-archical thinking.

When we categorize animals solely by their instrumental value, we may also be inclined to devote a lot of time and energy to controlling them to maximize their usefulness. Animals become tools we use to improve our lives. Although those species commonly kept as pets fare better than others, the denigration of animals and the natural world—and our desire to control both—appears to be ubiquitous in the modern West. It may even be an unavoidable aspect of human nature.

## The Control of Nature

In the book *Dominance and Affection: The Making of Pets*, human geographer Yi-Fu Tuan explores the thesis that humans have an innate need to dominate and control the natural world.[13] Tuan asserts that this need is sometimes expressed aggressively, as when we clear-cut forests and natural habitats to make room for human development. But our need to dominate nature is also expressed in behavior that is cloaked in terms of affection, aesthetics, play, and pleasure. This is where pets enter the picture. As Tuan writes, "Dominance may be cruel and exploitative, with no hint of affection in it. What it produces is the victim. On the other hand, dominance may be combined with affection, and what it produces is the pet."[14]

Tuan offers numerous examples, both historical and contemporary, to support his thesis that our desire to keep pets is grounded in an obsessive need to control the environment and everything in it. We take pleasure in manipulating animals physically to promote certain qualities, such as a hunting dog's acute sense of smell or a racehorse's long legs. Yet selective breeding does not consistently benefit the ani-mals we control. English bulldogs have been bred to have large heads, but puppies can only be delivered by C-section because their heads are too big for a normal birth. Similarly, pugs have been bred to have flat faces that resemble those of human infants, but this popular breed often has breathing issues because their nasal cavities are so narrow. Many other full-bred dogs develop hip dysplasia or other chronic health problems due to excessive breeding.

Some people understandably find Tuan's observations about human nature harsh, claiming he ignores people's genuine love for their animals and the natural world. Yet the evidence he presents to support his ideas is hard to argue with. As a species, human beings relish displays of power over animals. Animals have long been used by royalty and other wealthy, powerful people to demonstrate their prowess, such as the menageries of wild animals—often shackled, chained, and caged—that were displayed by the nobility. This practice was common worldwide in the premodern era, including in far-flung empires such as China and Western Europe that had little contact with each other, indicating that these behaviors are not unique to just one culture. Circuses and trophy hunting satisfy the same need today, and people who keep exotic animals like lions and tigers as pets also enjoy controlling animals who could kill them in an instant (and sometimes do).

Thankfully, our partnerships with animals are sometimes truly beneficial to both animals and ourselves. Working dogs such as border collies need to work to be happy, and these dogs and their handlers enjoy collaborating toward a common goal. Yet where do we draw the line? Do we consistently consider the impact of our behavior on the animals we claim to care for? Definitely not. In supporting his thesis that even pampered pets suffer at the hands of their human guardians, Tuan describes a scene from a dog obedience show, which he states is an example of "refined cruelty":

> Perhaps the hardest test required that the dog should be brought into the ring hungry, and when given a plate of his favorite food, sit by it until he was told to eat; the time was four minutes, and the owner had to go out of sight, leaving the dog alone with his tempting plate. Hundreds of people were watching when, on one occasion, Beeswing [a tiny Pekinese]

came into the ring. He was ravenous, and the four minutes must have seemed interminable; he endured for two and then, without moving from his post, slowly got up and, in Miss Cynthia's words, "sat on his bottom and begged." The crowd roared but he did not move a muscle. He had not broken the rules, but instead of sitting on four legs sat on two; after another two minutes, the judge called her; Beeswing saw his mistress come into the ring but knew he still must not move as she walked up and stood beside him. She had to wait for the word from the judge. It came, she released Beeswing, who literally jumped on the food and gobbled it.[15]

If we're honest, we must admit that we dominate the animals in our lives even as our hearts swell with love for them. Most pet keepers describe their animals as family members and believe their relationships with their pets are mutually beneficial, yet these relationships are certainly not equal. We are, by necessity, the guardians and caregivers of the animals we bring into our homes. For centuries, animals commonly kept as pets, such as dogs and cats, have been bred to be passive creatures, and the characteristics that we value in them as companions—docility and an eagerness to please us—have come at the expense of their ability to fend for themselves without our care. Pets depend on us for their basic needs (food, water, and shelter), and most lack the agency to move about freely or decide how they spend their time. Person-pet relationships are unequal because we have far more power over our pets than they have over us, despite the testimony of pet keepers who claim their animals rule the roost.

In the next chapter, we'll continue our study of the human-animal bond with a focus on person-pet relationships as we consider two essential questions: How does the bond benefit us, and how does it benefit our pets? Though these would appear to be simple queries, the answers are not as straightforward as you might believe.

# CHAPTER 2

# A Mutually Beneficial Relationship?

When I was about twelve years old, I liked to hang out with a group of friends in my hometown of Schaghticoke, a small village located north of Troy in upstate New York. A stray dog used to follow us, begging for a bit of whatever treat we might have in our pockets. Someone said the dog's name was Rex, but nobody knew where he came from. He was a homeless street urchin, scrawny, dirty, and always hungry. I wanted nothing to do with him.

One day, when I got home after hanging out with my friends, I walked into our living room to find some of my brothers and sisters watching TV. To my surprise, there was Rex. He had been washed and brushed and was curled up in front of the TV on my mother's handmade braided rug. I couldn't believe it. I remember feeling embarrassed. In my mind, Rex was a worthless scavenger. Looking around at my siblings, I asked with no small amount of incredulity, "Rex is our dog now?!" There was silence.

I knew it was my mom who had rescued Rex. A big-time animal lover, she was always leaving food out on our back stoop for the strays who wandered by. I loved all our pets, but I wasn't happy about Rex's unexpected arrival. To me, he was a nuisance—a loathsome wanderer that we kids made of and sometimes teased. I also thought we already had a full house. With Rex in the picture, we had three dogs, three or four cats, an untold number of gerbils, plus six kids and my mom and dad.

But early one winter morning, Rex completely upended my assumptions about him. It was around 3 a.m. when he began barking incessantly, waking up the whole house with his racket. My father yelled at him to be quiet, but Rex kept right on barking, which was odd because he was usually quiet. My father eventually went downstairs to see what the matter was. He later told us that Rex was in the kitchen in the back of the house, barking at a door that led to a storage room where we kept canned goods and household cleaners. When my father opened the door to investigate, he found a small fire caused by faulty electrical wiring.

From that day on, we called Rex our "wonder dog." He was our hero. He'd resisted all efforts to quiet him because he knew something was wrong. I was convinced he was the smartest dog I'd ever known.

My memories of Rex are precious to me now. Near the end of his life, it occurred to me that I might need forgiveness for callously letting him roam the streets and rejecting him when my mother first took him in. But it never seemed to matter to Rex that I had judged him. After he became my family's hero and I began treating him with respect and affection, his behavior toward me never changed. He wagged his tail when he greeted me from the day he came to live in our home until the day he died years after I had left for college. He forgave me for my early transgressions quickly and completely.

Rex taught me some important lessons, and when I reflect on my experiences with him, I realize that his story illustrates a core principle of the human-animal bond as it is currently defined—that these relationships are, by definition, *mutually beneficial.* Rex benefited greatly when he became a member of my family. He no longer roamed the streets, scrounging for food and getting chased by insensitive children. He was loved and doted upon, as were all the animals and children in my home. My family members and I also benefited greatly from Rex's presence. He was loyal and fiercely protective of his new pack, and he ultimately saved our home and perhaps even our lives.

The phrase *human-animal bond* was coined in the 1977 by veterinarian Leo Bustad and psychiatrist Michael McCulloch, who were among the founding members of the Delta Society. Known today as Pet Partners, the nonprofit's mission is to "improve human health and well-being through the human-animal bond."[1] The American Veterinary Medical Association (AVMA) defines the human-animal bond as "a mutually beneficial and dynamic relationship between people and animals that is influenced by behaviors essential to the health and well-being of both. This includes, among other things, emotional, psychological, and physical interactions of people, animals, and the environment."[2] The term is typically used to describe our relationships with those species commonly kept as pets: the cats, dogs, rodents, horses, birds, fish, reptiles, and other animals whom we consider to be valued members of our families.

Many person-pet relationships are mutually beneficial, like the friendship my family and I enjoyed with Rex. Indeed, many pets are pampered and well cared for throughout their lives. Animals can now receive hip replacements, kidney transplants, and advanced cancer treatments, and be prescribed antidepressants. In the pet food aisle at the grocery store, we can choose food produced with ethical farming practices, organic ingredients, and probiotics, as well as specialized food blends for young and old animals, overweight and underweight animals, and animals with allergies and illnesses such as diabetes.

Given such trends, you might say to yourself, "Anthropocentrism? Are you crazy?" Many pets live more comfortable and less stressful lives than their people, and they also eat better.

Yet the human-animal bond scales presented in the last chapter show that even those species commonly kept as pets don't consistently benefit from their interactions with us. In this chapter, we'll explore the many ways that people benefit from the human-animal bond, and we'll also explore how animals benefit. True reciprocity appears to be relatively rare, even in our relationships with our pets. Research into the human-animal bond has been ongoing for nearly fifty years, yet we still have a limited understanding of how our interactions with our pets impact them. This discrepancy is due in part to the difficulty of gauging what animals think and feel. Yet it is also true that researchers are only beginning to explore this vital question, and what research has been done suggests that the bonds we share with our animal companions are not consistently as mutually beneficial as we believe.

## How the Bond Benefits Humans

In *Always in My Heart*, the second book in the Pet Chaplain Learning Series, I explored the many benefits we enjoy in the company of our pets. This includes nonjudgmental love and forgiveness; a healing presence and physical closeness; constancy; and joy and play, among others. Our animal companions serve as important attachment figures in our lives, and a trusting relationship with a pet can boost our self-esteem and satisfy our basic need to be loved.[3] People who work with therapy animals assert that relationships with animals like dogs or horses are safe and straightforward, with minimal risk, because animals are often accepting, openly affectionate, honest, loyal, and consistent.[4] In the following passage, social work scholar Froma Walsh summarizes the findings of decades of research into the human-animal bond:

> Above all, [people] value their [pets for their] companion-
> ship, pleasure, and affection. Pets respond eagerly to care
> and attention, offering unconditional love and nonthreaten-
> ing physical contact in holding and petting—crucial human
> needs. Attachments with pets provide psychological and
> social support. After a stressful workday, their enthusiastic
> greeting, affection, and nonjudgmental support lead many,
> on arriving home, to prefer the company of their pets to that
> of their spouses! . . . While most families report that their pet

is of great importance to them at all times, they value them
most at times of crisis and loss, through disruptive transitions,
and in weathering prolonged adversity. . . . When [human
family] members are feeling vulnerable, lonely, or depressed,
others may be preoccupied, distant, or uncomfortable in
relating. Bonds with pets offer comfort, affection, and a sense
of security.[5]

In the early 1990s, a new field of therapy called Animal Assisted
Interventions (AAI) began to emerge when the Delta Society developed the first comprehensive certification program for animal-assisted
activities and therapy. In 2005 the American Psychological Association
(APA) established a division dedicated exclusively to AAI research and
practice. Therapy animals are now regularly brought into hospitals,
hospices, nursing homes, prisons, and mental health facilities. They're
also frequent visitors in non-medical settings, such as primary schools,
universities, and community programs (e.g., elder day care and af-
ter-school care). Specially trained animals are also increasingly used by
disaster response teams to support people who've experienced trauma.

Because of their calming influence, animals are used to treat
conditions that are caused or exacerbated by stress, including allergies
and immunity disorders; cancer; cardiovascular disease; Alzheimer's
disease and other types of dementia; autism; post-traumatic stress
disorder (PTSD); and depression and anxiety. Others who benefit
from AAI include those recovering from alcohol or substance abuse,
violence and abuse survivors, and underserved or marginalized youth.
For people who suffer from mental illness, pets improve their ability
to feel joy and pleasure; motivate them to get up and move around
every day to care for their pet; reduce their anxiety and panic attacks;
improve their social connections; soothe their feelings of loneliness;
and reduce risky behaviors (e.g., self-harming or suicide ideation).[6]

So what is the secret behind animals' ability to soothe and heal us?
Using powerful brain-imaging technology, neuroscientists have begun

to unlock the physiological reasons animals make us feel so good and help us recover faster from our physical ailments. They've discovered, for example, that positive feelings carry a unique chemical signature in the brain. Images of human and animal babies alike trigger the release of dopamine and oxytocin, the same chemicals that are released when people fall in love, have sex, or take drugs.[7] A similar chemical dance takes place when we stroke our pets. Both people and furred pets have sensory neurons on their skin called *C-tactile afferents*. Gently stroking these neurons stimulates the release of oxytocin.[8] Touching also releases internal opiates such as endorphins, which are commonly referred to as the happiness hormone because they increase good feelings and reduce pain.

Dogs are the leaders of the pack among animal health-care providers. In addition to their calming influence, dogs use their keen senses to detect seizures and migraines before they occur, giving affected people a window of opportunity to reach a safe place or manage their condition. They can also detect high and low blood sugar levels in people with diabetes and sniff out cancer, urinary tract infections, and diseases such as tuberculosis. Horses are also commonly used for AAI, especially with autistic and traumatized children.

Cats are typically not used in formal AAI work, but they offer many health benefits to their human companions. Watching funny cat videos is relaxing. But did you know that the vibration of a cat's purr can reduce inflammation and heal strained tendons? A purr's vibration ranges from 20 to 140 megahertz, a frequency known to be medically therapeutic for many illnesses.[9] According to neurologist Dr. Jean-Marc Aimonetti, "The cat, like all mammals, perceives low frequencies thanks to sensors located in his skin, called Pacini corpuscles. These detectors transform feline vibrations into electrical impulses and transmit them to the [cat's] brain, which responds by secreting endorphins."[10] Humans possess the same Pacini corpuscles, so people and cats alike enjoy the soothing benefits of a cat's purr. Being in the presence of a happy, purring cat can lower your blood pressure, reduce your risk of heart disease, and boost your immune system.[11]

Exotic species have also been brought into the AAI fold. In an article in *The New York Times Magazine,* journalist Charles Seibert describes an innovative animal therapy program that matches rescued parrots with people suffering from PTSD.[12] Many of the parrots in the program were captured in the wild and sold illegally in the US before being relinquished or abandoned by their keepers or rescued from neglectful or abusive situations. The traumatized parrots and people are helping each other heal. In the words of one program participant, the parrots' "spirit gives me the will to get up and do it another day. They're all victims here. Kind of like what the veterans have been through, in a way. . . . I see the trauma, the mutual trauma that I suffered and that these birds have suffered, and my heart just wants to go out and nurture and feed and take care of them, and doing that helps me deal with my trauma. All without words."[13]

In addition to the many health benefits that animals offer us, they also improve our social lives. This is especially true for dog enthusiasts, who often get to know their neighbors on their daily walks with their canine friends. People stop and chat while their dogs mill around, wagging their tails and sniffing each other in the standard doggy way of saying hello. Dogs make their human companions more socially attractive to others, stimulating conversation and friendly behaviors from strangers.[14]

Pet keepers are fully aware of these benefits. Most say they keep pets in part because it's good for their health. No matter what kind of animal they have—dogs, cats, horses, small rodents, birds, fish, and reptiles—80 percent of pet keepers derive happiness and emotional support from their animals, and most also report lower levels of stress, anxiety, and depression.[15] Nearly 90 percent of dog or cat lovers say their pets have a positive impact on their mental health, and the same proportion considers their pets to be valued members of their families.[16] When asked who listens to them best, almost half of the respondents to a nationwide survey chose a pet, while only a third chose a spouse or significant other.[17]

For many of us, our animals serve as an antidote to the stresses of modern life, rather like a personal live-in therapist for whatever ails us. Pet keeping is fun, improves our health, and helps us weather the ups and downs of life. It's no wonder so many of us are jumping on the pet-keeping train and discovering that pets are far more than "just animals."

## How the Bond Benefits Animals

Among people who keep pets, I expect it seems obvious that our pets enjoy many benefits from their relationships with us. Like us, animals crave creature comforts: a warm place to sleep, nutritious and plentiful food, and a family to hang out with. Dogs are highly social animals descended from wolves, who live in complex social groups, so our canine friends treat us like members of their pack. They enjoy playing with us, sitting on our laps, getting belly rubs, snuggling under the covers, and basically going everywhere we go.

Cats, who are independent animals in the wild, are more selective in their displays of affection, but their slow-blinking stares, musical purrs, kneading, and stroke-seeking behavior attest to the pleasure they receive from us. Researchers from Oregon State University found that cats exhibit the same attachment to their keepers as kittens do to their mothers.[18] The kittens acted distressed when their caregivers left and became happy, playful, and secure when they returned. They still acted this way one year later. The study authors noted that these responses are remarkably similar to how children respond to their parents.

Notably, however, of the hundreds of studies of person-pet relationships that HAS researchers have conducted over the last thirty years, almost all have focused exclusively on the ways that animals help people. Only a handful have attempted to evaluate whether interacting with people benefits or harms animals.[19] I recently did a Google Scholar search on how an animal's relationship with a human affects the animal, and I was astonished by the paucity of the results. Almost all the chatter in the academic world about the wonders of the human-animal bond focuses on how people benefit with no thought to how animals benefit—or don't benefit—from their relationships with us.

Although my research was not exhaustive, I found only a few studies that examined the impact of human interaction on animals commonly kept as pets. Most of these were completed in the last decade, such as the study that examined the effects of purring on cats' physiology, which was completed in 2019.[20] Historically, the earliest study of the physiological effects of petting on dogs was conducted in 1966, using laboratory animals as subjects.[21] This study found that the dogs' heart rates increased when a person entered the room without interacting with the dog but decreased when the dogs were petted. Thirty years later, a Japanese study showed that horses respond well to gentle stroking.[22] Both studies affirm that animals enjoy many of the same physiological benefits from the human-animal bond that we enjoy, such as lowered heart rates and reduced stress.

In the absence of empirical research, how do we know if animals benefit from their relationships with us? We can't ask our animals what they think and feel about being a pet or what they would change about their lives if they could. Animal behaviorists help us understand the physical cues our pets give us about their emotional state, which can guide our behavior (more on this later in the chapter). On a broad scale, however, the best we can do is to examine typical pet-keeping practices and map them against our understanding of a particular species' needs.

This was precisely the purpose of a study from researchers at Wichita State University, which offers some interesting insights into the daily lives of American pets.[23] The study found that almost all pets lead relatively comfortable lives in the company of their human companions, with sufficient food, water, shelter, and veterinary care. However, what the researchers described as "essential care" does not necessarily translate into a good quality of life. A dog may have food and water, but spend their days confined in a small apartment or tied up in a yard with little social interaction. Notably, the study found that only about a third of pets receive what the researchers described as "enhanced care," including daily playtime with their human companion, regular exercise, and freedom to move throughout the home.

In a society where almost all pet keepers say their pet is a member of the family, you might expect the proportion of pets who are truly treated as family members—with all the benefits that this implies—to be higher. It seems that how we define what it means for a pet to be a family member is different for different people. I'm not saying that animals who spend most of their time outside are unhappy or mistreated. Most are much better adapted than humans to living outside, given reasonable conditions. Beyond the basics of food, water, and shelter, what most animals need more than anything is consistent social interaction, exercise, and the freedom to engage in natural behaviors.

And what about service animals? To date, only a few studies have examined the impact of therapy work on the animals who provide these services. Though limited, this research offers mixed results, with most studies finding that therapy work takes a toll on animals. A US study found that therapy dogs showed no adverse physical responses to their work, with no changes in heart rate, salivary cortisol and oxytocin levels, or ear temperature.[24] But a European study found that the levels of stress hormones on dogs' tongues after an hour-long visit to a hospital were elevated but remained unchanged after a visit to a college dorm room.[25] The researchers attributed the difference to the unpredictability of a hospital setting, which seems reasonable given the constant beeping of machines and the high stress that is common among hospitalized people. Another US study found that inappropriate behavior, such as teasing visiting dogs, was observed in AAI recipients and staff members at hospitals or other institutions where the therapy took place.[26] The same study also found that therapy dogs who work with children with multiple disabilities had to be terminated early because of the adverse impact on the dogs' health as evidenced by symptoms of stress like excessive panting and tiredness.

In the book *Our Wild Calling: How Connecting with Animals Can Transform Our Lives—and Save Theirs*, Richard Louv tells the story of a therapy dog named Koba, a standard poodle who was an autistic teenager's companion.[27] For the girl, Naomi, the benefits of the relationship were clear. "We're so bonded that I know what he's thinking and feeling, and he knows what I'm thinking and feeling," she said.[28] Naomi occasionally suffered panic attacks in busy public spaces. Koba could sense these attacks before they came and was trained to nudge Naomi or lie down on top of her until she calmed down. For Koba, absorbing Naomi's chaotic energy was hard work, and it took a toll. As Louv notes, "These dogs are not robots."[29] Because their work is so demanding, service dogs like Koba typically work for eight to ten years, at which point they're permitted to engage only in short sessions with mildly autistic children or retire altogether. Some service dogs are adopted by their original keepers, but this is not always possible if the person who needs the support lives in a facility that doesn't allow pets or cannot afford to keep more than one animal. Ending these close relationships can be traumatic for both the people and their service animals. As one woman noted about the loss of her therapy dog shortly after he retired, "The dog's whole life has had purpose. The dog puts on a harness and does a job. To be without the harness—it can be devastating for the dog."[30]

Many service animals appear to enjoy their work, but they can also experience emotional burnout, as can people who work in helping professions.[31] Experts in animal therapy advise people with service animals to give their companions frequent breaks and opportunities to relieve the stress they pick up on the job. "It is my ethical responsibility to ensure the safety and well-being of my dog," writes Amy Johnson, an AAI specialist. "This means balancing not only the values of [the

AAI] profession and operating within our scopes of practice but having a solid understanding of my dog's needs."[32]

We love to celebrate the incredible gifts of animals like Koba and the wonderful benefits we enjoy because of their loving and steadfast support. We don't like to think we're using these animals for our benefit, because the term implies that these relationships are transactional. Yet Koba is a working animal, and in this way, he is no different from dogs selectively bred for service as guards, herders, and hunters. He is meeting a different human need, one that's emotional rather than utilitarian

. . .

The human-animal bond can be a beautiful thing, characterized by mutual care and respect. Yet it's also incredibly complex. Driven by the need to control the natural world, we sometimes subjugate our animal companions even as we love them. With their generous spirits and loving hearts, our animals sometimes make big sacrifices to meet our needs, and we don't always return that love in kind. As noted earlier, not all person-pet relationships in America qualify as mutually beneficial, which requires careful attention to animals' needs beyond the basics of food, water, and shelter.

Despite the growing popularity of pet keeping in Western society, millions of people appear to regard animals with indifference or even contempt. Others claim to like animals but don't regularly interact with them and don't spend much time thinking about them. As we saw in chapter 1, most people think about animals solely in terms of their instrumental value. Yet we bristle at the notion of categorizing humans in the same way. It's as if we've constructed a giant wall between ourselves and the rest of the animal kingdom. Although *homo sapiens* are animals, we typically don't refer to ourselves as animals. This strikes me as a peculiar aspect of human nature, and I've done a lot of research into this phenomenon. The answers I found surprised me, and they may surprise you as well.

CHAPTER 3

# I Am Not an Animal!

Scientists long ago established the genetic link between humans and other primates, but many of us don't really think of ourselves as animals. When referring to human beings, we use the pronoun *who*, but for animals, we use the pronouns *that* and *it*, which are typically reserved for inanimate objects. In addition, we often say "humans and nonhuman animals," a phrase that implies people are not animals, rather than saying "humans and other animals." As primatologist Frans de Waal quips, "The term *nonhuman* grates on me, since it lumps millions of species together by an absence, as if they were missing something. Poor things, they are nonhuman!"[1]

We also express our contempt for animals and our dominance over them in everyday conversation. There are, after all, many ways to skin a cat. Don't beat a dead horse or you might end up in the doghouse, and you can always maximize your efficiency by killing two birds with one stone. You get the idea.

Even worse, when we want to express how badly a person is being oppressed or bullied, we say they're being treated "like an animal," a phrase that makes me cringe because it implies that there is something reasonable about mistreating an animal. Similarly, the word *animality* would appear to be a straightforward way of denoting the state of being an animal, or "a quality or nature associated with animals," according to *Merriam-Webster*.[2] Yet *animality* is a loaded term, and its synonyms—words like *brutishness, viciousness, savagery*, and *malevolence*—reveal the powerful anti-animal bias at work in our culture.[3]

Talking about animals in a derogatory way is so commonplace that most of us don't give it a second thought. Taken to an extreme, however, the beliefs that drive our linguistic habits can lead to radical conclusions. Gary Kurz, a pet lover who has written several books on animals and the afterlife, captures this sentiment when he writes, "God made . . . animals after their own kind. They were not made in His image, only mankind was. [Animals] will never turn into you or me. I do not like being referred to as a mammal. I am not a mammal. I am not an animal. I am a man. None of my ancestors hung from a tree by their tail. Some may have hung by their necks, but never by their tails."[4] Yes, Kurz loves his pets, but he also draws a hard line between himself and his animal friends.

In keeping with our self-aggrandizing perspective, our culture demands that we avoid behaving like the animals we are. Even if we acknowledge that we're animals, we tell ourselves that we're *civilized* animals. Yet beneath the veneer of our civilized selves, we are still animals. And beneath the cloak of our civility lies a deep-seated anxiety about our own mortality.

Now, you might be wondering what our habit of denigrating animals has to do with death. But there is a connection, and understanding this connection can provide insight into the psychological roots of the human-centered worldview that dominates Western culture and, indeed, the entire human race.

To explicate these ideas, I'll turn to the work of the late Ernest Becker, an American cultural anthropologist whose seminal book, *The Denial of Death*, was awarded the Pulitzer Prize in 1974.[5] Becker addresses a simple but complex question: Why do people do what they do? After years of study, this query led Becker to conclude that our unconscious fear of our own mortality drives our behavior. Our anxiety about death manifests in countless ways in our lives, and one of those ways is our habit of drawing a sharp division between humans and other animals.

## Out of Nature and Hopelessly in It

Becker's theories about human death anxiety begin with a simple fact: All life on this planet eventually dies. Physical immortality is impossible. Because we humans are acutely aware of our imminent demise, we need to find a way to manage the terror that our awareness of our mortality evokes.

Culture is our answer to this dilemma. The whole of human culture, as Becker frames it, is an expression of humankind's efforts to deny death. Culture enables us to meet our fundamental need to maintain psychological equanimity despite our awareness of our mortality. Through a variety of cultural activities, we continually strive for more life and maintain hope that our legacies continue after our physical bodies cease to function. By "cultural activities," I'm referring to everything from religion and spiritual practices to science, technology, art, literature, and other creative endeavors. The stories we tell about the afterlife, the buildings we erect, the music, paintings, sculptures, books, and poems we create, the history we write, and the inventions we devise survive our deaths and give us a sense of meaning and purpose. Of all the cultural activities we engage in to achieve immortality, religion is one of the most powerful because all religious traditions and many alternative spiritual practices promise that life continues after death in a spiritual realm.

The things we do to quell our anxiety about our mortality can be beautiful and life-affirming. In fact, *any* activity we engage in to find meaning and purpose in life is ultimately a response to our unconscious worries about our own mortality. We gravitate toward activities that boost our self-esteem and help us leave a legacy we can be proud of. Rescuing and healing animals are excellent examples of a life-affirming response to death. They represent a meaningful way to contribute to society, and for many of the people who engage in this work, they're deeply spiritual acts.

Unfortunately, we also manage our death anxiety in negative and potentially harmful ways, which brings us back to the focus of this chapter. Although many people in the modern West are passionate about animals, our society as a whole doesn't have a stellar record when it comes to animals. According to Becker, the anthropocentric paradigm that drives our behavior is rooted in our unconscious fear of death. He asserts that humankind is trapped in a paradox because we're both "out of nature and hopelessly in it. We're aware of our "own splendid uniqueness in that [we] stick out of nature with a towering majesty, and yet [we] go back into the ground . . . blindly and dumbly to disappear forever. It is a terrifying dilemma to be in and to have to live with."[6] In response to this dilemma, we separate ourselves from animals in countless ways. We categorize them according to their usefulness; other them with our words; demean their intelligence and emotional lives; erect physical barriers that keep wild animals from encroaching into our cities, suburbs, and dwellings; and eradicate unwanted species to suit our needs and make way for the continuous growth of human civilization.

Of course, our pets are an important exception to this trend. Most people consider their animals to be valued members of their families, and many pets lead comfortable, carefree lives. Yet as discussed in the last chapter, even as we love our pets, we sometimes unwittingly ask too much of them. We also control many aspects of their daily lives and deny them the ability to live according to their own wishes. More importantly, we unconsciously separate ourselves from them, especially when they behave like the messy, mortal creatures that they are—slobbering, defecating, shedding, licking their privates, and fornicating without shame. Our dogs and cats are also hunters equipped with sharp teeth and claws that helped their ancestors survive in the wild. When your dog attacks a neighbor's cat or your feline friend leaves the gift of a mangled bird on your doorstep, they're simply being the animals they are. Yet when we witness such behavior, we sometimes cringe in embarrassment or turn away in disgust.

Human beings also engage in these activities. We are, after all, the world's most successful predator. But we keep these aspects of ourselves under tight control, hidden behind closed doors or channeled into hunting, competitive and sometimes brutal team sports, violent movies and video games, warfare, and other culturally acceptable expressions of aggression. We also work hard to hide or mask our creatureliness. Removing unwanted body hair in many cultures stems at least in part from our unexamined desire to erase our animal-ness. Perfumes and deodorants serve the same purpose. Such activities may seem like harmless aesthetic preferences, yet these habits and countless others reinforce our belief that we are not base animals.

The bottom line is that animals threaten our desire to escape our fates as bleeding, defecating, messy, fragile, utterly mortal beings, and we respond to this perceived threat by controlling, denigrating, and commodifying them. When we think about animals solely as objects, we strengthen the wall we've built between us. In this passage from *Escape from Evil*, Becker clarifies the connection between our fear of death and the oppression of animals: "Mortality is connected to the natural, animal side of [human] existence; and so man reaches beyond and away from that side. So much so that he tries to deny it completely. As soon as man reached new historical forms of power, he turned against the animals with whom he had previously identified—with a vengeance, as we now see, because the animals embodied what man feared most, a nameless and faceless death."[7]

The sad irony is that the separation we've created between ourselves and other animals has led to many unanticipated and unwelcome consequences. This separation has done great harm to animals, the natural world, and, ultimately to ourselves. As Becker scholars Michael Mountain and Lori Marino write, "The deterioration of our relationship with other animals, the damage we inflict on the natural world, and the inevitable harm this has on our own lives are inextricably linked to our insistence that 'I am not an animal!'"[8]

## Proving Becker's Theory

It can be difficult to fully appreciate the connection between our habitual denigration of animals and our deep-seated anxiety about death. But it's important to remember that Becker asserts that death anxiety is *unconscious*. As we go about our daily lives, we're simply not aware that our terror of death is rattling around deep in our psyche, shaping our beliefs and daily choices.

If you're skeptical about these ideas, you're not alone. In the mid-1980s, about ten years after the publication of Becker's *The Denial of Death*, three social psychologists who had studied Becker's ideas—Sheldon Solomon, Jeff Greenberg, and Tom Pyszczynski—introduced his theories to their fellow scholars at an academic conference. They were met with a lot of skepticism. Becker's theories, they were told, were compelling, but they wouldn't be taken seriously in the academic world unless they could be empirically proven. Becker's theory of death anxiety predicts that people respond in culturally prescribed ways when reminded of their own mortality. But is this actually the case? Is our behavior so predictable? And, for our purposes, how can we credibly link our habitual denigration of animals to an *unconscious* anxiety of death?

In the book *The Worm at the Core*, Solomon, Greenberg, and Pyszczynski tell the story of their efforts to scientifically prove to their fellow academics (and to the world) that Becker's theory of death anxiety could be empirically verified.[9] The trio eventually devised some ingenious experiments that demonstrated a causal link between our unconscious anxiety about death and our behavior. Since their first study in 1989, hundreds of studies have been completed in a new branch of psychology known as "terror management." The results of these studies have been remarkably consistent. People do, in fact, respond in predictable, culturally prescribed ways to reminders of death, or what is called a *death prime*. Such responses occur when those reminders are overt, as when a study participant is asked to write a short essay about death before completing a challenging task. But these reminders can also be subliminal, as when an image of a dead body, a cemetery, or words associated with death is flashed for milliseconds on a computer screen, a time frame too brief for our conscious minds to register. When reminded of death in these ways, we become more committed to our own worldview, certain that our perspective is the only one that is true and valid. We cling more tightly to our social groups and criticize people who don't share our worldview.

Death anxiety, then, can be appreciated as a hidden driver for many kinds of behavior, from relatively innocuous things such as avoiding stepping on cracks in the sidewalk to the most extreme acts of cruelty in which one group of people attempts to eradicate others whose worldview challenges their own.

To return to the focus of this chapter, our death anxiety also drives our perspective about animals as well as the way we treat them. Studies have shown that a death prime can prompt us to take a more critical perspective toward animals than we usually do. In the book *How to Be Animal*, Melanie Challenger offers the example of a 2001 study of American college students that measured how their beliefs about animals shifted following a death prime.[10] Students were divided into two groups, one that received a death prime and a control group that did not. Each group was then presented with two different essays about animals with different content but the same title: "The Most Important Things I Have Learned About Human Nature." One essay argued that "the boundary between humans and animals is not as great as most people think. . . . Although we like to think that we are special and unique, our bodies work in pretty much the same way as the bodies of all other animals." The second essay claimed that "although we humans have some things in common with other animals, human beings are truly unique." This statement was followed by a long list of human accomplishments, from art and music to language and abstract thinking. The students who received a death prime before reading these essays consistently showed a strong preference for the version that emphasized human uniqueness compared to the essay on human creatureliness. The students who did not receive a death prime showed no such preference.

Other studies have documented similar trends among people who keep pets. Psychologist Ruth Beatson gave two groups of volunteer pet keepers two different primes—one that reminded them of their own mortality and another that reminded them of their creatureliness, or their similarity to other animals.[11] Before and after receiving these primes, participants were asked to complete a series of questions in which they rated the good and negative qualities of other pets (not their personal pets); they were also questioned about their attitudes about treating pets like people, such as taking a dog to a pet spa. Participants in both groups exhibited more negative attitudes toward pets following the mortality and creatureliness primes than before. The authors concluded that, as predicted, when pet keepers are prompted to reflect on their own mortality and creatureliness, they develop the same negative attitudes toward pets as toward other animals.

When it comes to their personal pets, however, people were not so negative. Beatson conducted a followup study to see if pet keepers' attitudes towards their *own* pets would show a similar shift following a mortality or creatureliness prime.[12] She discovered that following the death and creatureliness primes, the way pet keepers rated their own pets did not shift as much as it did when they were asked to rate an animal they didn't know or animals in general. Apparently, a loving relationship with a pet can help alleviate our unconscious fear of mortality and discomfort with our creatureliness.

## Death Anxiety and the Control of Nature

Becker's theory of death anxiety and its connection to the denigration and oppression of animals in the modern world raises an interesting question. If death anxiety is common to all human beings and transcends time, place, and culture, how do we account for cultures that don't systematically denigrate and oppress animals?

In pondering this query, it's important to remember that death anxiety is expressed in ways that are specific to a particular culture. People in ancient tribal societies who were in constant contact with animals and the natural world sought to learn from animals. They hunted them for food, but they also deified animals who possessed powers they did not, such as birds who could fly or fierce predators who could kill them with their teeth, claws, hooves, or venom. These beliefs reflect the reality of their daily lives, and people in these societies sought different ways to express their death anxiety. Sometimes this involved sacrificing people and animals to propitiate the gods and keep evil spirits at bay, but there's little evidence that ancient tribal peoples systematically objectified, controlled, and oppressed animals as we do today.

Similarly, the denigration and oppression of animals that pervades the modern world reflects the reality of our lives, where natural resources are being quickly depleted and competition for arable land is fierce. *All* modern cultures commodify and oppress animals to one degree or another. Some societies, like some people, are more oppressive than others, but the consumption of animal products and resource extraction is rising worldwide as human civilizations continue to grow and expand into areas that used to be home to relatively untouched wilderness.

In chapter 2, we learned that humans are strongly inclined to control the natural world. In *Dominance and Affection*, Yi-Fu Tuan methodically documented the sometimes loving, sometimes destructive ways that humans manipulate other life forms and the earth itself.[13] In this chapter, we explored Ernest Becker's theory that our inclination to denigrate animals and separate ourselves from them is rooted in our unconscious anxiety about our own mortality. Is there a connection between these two ideas? I believe there is. While Becker's ideas address the unconscious impulses that drive our controlling behavior, Tuan's work addresses the outward expression of those impulses.

The point is that death anxiety and the expression of that anxiety through cultural activities appear to be an innate aspect of human nature. We cannot entirely control our need to dominate the world around us, including the animals in our midst. Yet I believe it's possible to deliberately choose a different perspective about animals and the natural world than the one mainstream culture provides. As noted by Becker scholar Daniel Liechty, Becker's ideas can help us see death "as an ally in life, an ally that helps [us] cut through the vanities of standardized cultural heroism, to recognize and concentrate on what is really important."[14]

Changing the way we think about ourselves and our attitudes toward animals begins with a critical perspective on the cultural norms to which we've become accustomed. In today's rapidly changing world, we tend to be very forward-thinking, and it can be difficult to appreciate how much our present reality is linked to our past. I've heard it said that it does no good to look to the past because that's not where we're going. But I believe otherwise. The path we've already traveled and the path ahead are part of the same journey, so to know where we're going, we must clearly understand where we've been. In the next chapter, I'll offer a brief history of Western culture with a focus on the core ideas that have guided our beliefs about animals and shaped a culture that habitually objectifies and denigrates them.

# Discussion Questions

1. Chapter 1 introduced two human-animal-bond scales that depict animals in a hierarchy based on their usefulness to people. What are the benefits of these scales and what are the costs, both to people and to animals?

2. Chapter 1 also explored the possibility that we humans tend to focus solely on our own needs and concerns with little to no consideration of the needs and concerns of other living beings or the earth itself, a perspective known as *anthropocentrism*. Describe where you stand on this concept and provide evidence for your position. For example, do you believe that we're justified in feeling superior to other animals and using animals to meet our wants and needs? Why or why not?

3. Chapter 2 explored how the human-animal bond benefits animals and people. How do you think people benefit from their relationships with pets, and how do you think pets benefit from their relationships with us? Reflect on your personal experiences with animals and provide examples to support your answer.

4. Chapter 2 also described the work of Yi-Fu Tuan, who asserts that humans habitually dominate or manipulate the natural world, including animals. Tuan also claims that such "dominance may be cruel and exploitative, with no hint of affection in it. What it produces is the victim. On the other hand, dominance may be combined with affection, and what it produces is the pet." Do you agree or disagree with Tuan's ideas? What thoughts and emotions

arise for you when you reflect on his hypothesis? Provide examples to support your answer.

5. In chapter 3, we reviewed cultural anthropologist Ernest Becker's theory of death anxiety, which holds that our unconscious anxiety about death drives our behavior and shapes how we view other animals. What are your thoughts on this theory? What evidence do you see in your own life that either supports or refutes this theory?

# Looking Back to Move Forward

## CHAPTER 4

# Animals and Western Society: A Brief History of Ideas

My mother, Helen Gierka, regularly rescued stray animals who wandered by our home. In a family with ten kids and innumerable pets, food and resources were in short supply, but my mom somehow found a way to feed everyone and keep us all healthy and comfortable.

One stray we adopted was a cat we named Cricket. She was a delicate, gray-and-white tabby who took up residence on our back porch and soon after gave birth to two kittens. We tended to Cricket and her kittens as we did all the animals who were members of our family. But then one day, at the beginning of May, just before my eighth birthday, Cricket and her two kittens disappeared.

We didn't have to witness the crime to know who had likely committed the catnapping. Unlike my mom, my dad was not an animal lover, and he sometimes grumbled about all the animals in the house. It was easy to imagine my father dropping the kittens and Cricket in a sack, throwing the wiggling bundle in the back of his station wagon, and speeding off before anyone could catch him in the act. Everyone in the family was angry at my dad. But the catnapping was especially hard on my mom, who took her animal rescue work very seriously.

The day we discovered that Cricket and her kittens were missing, Mom went into action. She placed a classified ad in the local paper and dispatched my big brother Ricky and me to go around the neighborhood on our bicycles, tacking up homemade flyers to telephone poles and dropping them off at local businesses. We knew that Cricket and her kittens might already be dead—hit and killed by a car, maybe, or attacked by a dog. But the newspaper ad and those flyers gave us all a feeling of empowerment and hope.

One Saturday morning about a week after the cats disappeared, a big truck with a shiny red cab pulled up in front of our house. Its arrival was an exciting novelty that sent all of us kids bumping like demolition derby cars to the front porch, some of us clothed only in our underwear. The trucker, an older man with a stars-and-stripes bandanna tied around his head, was cradling a black kitten. The kitten clawed her way up the man's chest and onto his shoulders when my siblings and I crowded around, jumping and shouting. We were sure the kitten was one of Cricket's. She was black all over except for a heart-shaped patch of white on the back of her right foot. We called her Cupid.

The trucker told my mom that Cupid had somehow managed to climb into the cab of his truck when he was sleeping. He was parked near the steel mill across the Hudson River in Watervliet. He'd seen Mom's ad in the local paper and thought it was worth stopping in on his way out of town. Mom thanked the trucker and offered him a cup of coffee, but he tipped his cap and said he had to get on the road.

Three weeks later, Cricket showed up at our back door. She was emaciated and filthy but otherwise OK. I've always marveled that she made it home. The steel mill where the trucker was parked was at least five miles from our house, and she would have had to negotiate busy city streets and a long, narrow bridge to make it to our back door. We never did find out what had happened to Cricket's second kitten, and we grieved her loss. But we drew comfort from the fact that Cricket and Cupid had rejoined our family.

It's easy to frame my dad as the bad guy in this story. But I've come to realize that my father wasn't a heartless or cruel man. As the first-generation son of Polish immigrants, he was a gruff, no-nonsense guy who worked as a maintenance welder at a steel mill. While he tolerated the many animals in our home, I don't think he ever truly felt at peace in our crazy household. I don't condone his actions, but I've sometimes imagined how he must have felt coming home after a double shift in a hot, smoky, gritty steel mill to a noisy house filled with wild, half-dressed kids and a dozen or more cats, dogs, and rodents. When he carted Cricket and her kittens away, he was probably trying to clear a little space in his crowded, hectic home.

When I think back on Cricket's catnapping and other experiences with animals in my childhood, I realize that the conflicting beliefs about animals in my family represent a personal reenactment of competing perspectives about animals that have defined Western society for millennia. My mother, siblings, and I were on one side of the divide between humans and animals. For us, Cricket and her kittens were members of our family. But to my father, who sat squarely on the other side of the human-animal divide, those cats were smelly fur balls with an attitude.

Many people in Western society are like my father—indifferent to animals or sometimes contemptuous of them. As noted in chapter 1, people who feel this way believe that humans are innately superior to other animals and that our needs outweigh theirs. In this chapter, we'll explore the historical roots of our culture's anthropocentric paradigm with a focus on philosophy, religion, and science. The core ideas about people, animals, and nature that arose in these fields of human endeavor have directed our interactions with animals and the natural world for centuries. Although some of the concepts discussed here may seem archaic, they're nonetheless central to our cultural heritage. Understanding where these ideas came from can provide valuable insight into the status quo and help us envision the future we want to create.

This analysis is, by necessity, a greatly simplified account of a complex cultural story. As noted above, this discussion focuses on philosophy, religion, and science. Yet economics and the pursuit of wealth and power have also played a central role in how we think about and treat the animals in our midst, including our pets. Our modern capitalist system commodifies virtually everything, and this aggressive, profit-driven mindset has spread rapidly around the globe in the past century. However, it's beyond the scope of this book to fully explore the impact of economic and political forces on our anthropocentric paradigm. Instead, I've chosen to focus on the pivotal ideas that, together, form the ethical foundation of the West's human-first worldview.

Before we get started, I'd like to note that this discussion doesn't distinguish between animals traditionally kept as pets and all other animals. The distinctions we draw between different species of animals, like the human-animal bond scales presented in chapter 1, are a relatively recent phenomenon. Pet keeping doesn't occur in isolation from our beliefs and interactions with other species. Our modern love affair with our pets rests on an ancient and complex web of human interaction with all other animal species and the planet as a whole. The plight of a black rhinoceros facing extinction in Africa is ultimately the same plight as that of a healthy young pit bull euthanized at an animal shelter in the US. Their lives are simply not valued by humankind, at least not enough to change their fates.

## Divine Reason and the Great Chain of Being

Many of the core ideas that have had a big impact on the West's anthropocentric worldview originated in ancient Greece, primarily in the work of philosophers Plato and Aristotle, who lived and worked between three and four hundred years before the birth of Christ. At that time, Greek civilization was flourishing. The city of Athens was home to a wealthy, intellectual class whose members had a lot of free time because they didn't have to hunt, tend animals, grow food, or build their own homes to survive. Slavery was common in ancient Greece, and Greek society was highly stratified between the wealthy, educated classes and everyone else.

In Plato's time, schools for men from wealthy families were established, and their education was focused largely on the philosophical contemplation of the nature of reality, the natural world, the cosmos, and the divine. Aristotle was Plato's student and colleague for about two decades at Plato's Academy in Athens, which was founded in the 380s (BCE) as an institution for philosophical, scientific, and mathematical research and teaching.

As a philosopher, Plato envisioned a utopian realm of existence where perfect forms existed. He maintained that this utopian realm was beyond the awareness and understanding of ordinary people, but that philosophers might grasp these ideal forms through the exercise of reason. For Plato, the human faculty for reason was divine but not in the way most modern people conceive of the idea. The ancient Greeks were pagan and polytheistic. They saw gods everywhere in the natural world. They also believed that people could interact directly with the gods and that divine beings could easily morph between human and animal forms. The Greek gods represented the pinnacle of power and were considered perfect, yet their perfection was something human beings could strive for.

Plato's student, Aristotle, also believed that reason was a divine quality and humans were innately superior to animals by virtue of their rational minds. He created a detailed metaphysical conception of the world that he called *scala naturae*, which translates literally as "ladder of being." Also known as the Great Chain of Being, *scala naturae* is a hierarchical system that depicts all matter and life in the known universe. Aristotle placed human beings one step below the gods, followed in descending order by animals, plants, and minerals. Because animals were thought to lack the divine gift of reason, they were placed farther down the ladder than people. As noted by Greek scholar Richard Tarnas, Aristotle believed that "the divine intellect, of which each man has a potential share and which distinguishes man from other animals, is immortal and transcendent."[1]

Hence, for learned men like Plato and Aristotle, the quality that set human beings apart from all other animals was their superior intellect and, specifically, their gift of reason. The belief that reason is a superior way of understanding the world has held true in the Western world ever since, which is one of the reasons that science has flourished in our society.

More than three centuries after Plato and Aristotle developed their philosophies, a Jew named Jesus was born, and a worldview dominated by a perfect, all-powerful God began to gain strength in Western civilization. Despite significant differences in the spiritual beliefs of pagan Greeks and monotheistic Christians, the belief that the human faculty for reason placed people above their fellow creatures in the scheme of things endured and was promoted as a core tenet of the Christian faith.

## Rational Versus Sentient Souls

The adoption of Greek philosophy into the Christian canon is largely attributed to Aurelius Augustine, who lived and worked between three and four hundred years after the birth of Christ. A renowned Catholic bishop, theologian, and rhetorician, Augustine was a prolific writer who authored more than two hundred books and nearly a thousand sermons, letters, and other works. At a time when the power of the written word belonged solely to Christian theologians, he had a profound impact on the development of Christian doctrine. Augustine's work served as a bridge between the pagan, polytheistic worldview of the ancient Greeks and the emerging monotheistic worldview of ascendant Christianity. In addition to his unwavering devotion to the contemplation and writing of Christian teachings, Augustine was an advocate of Neoplatonism, which as the name implies promoted

Plato's vision of a perfect realm and ideals of perfection that all human beings could aspire to.

Like Aristotle, Augustine argued that animals could not aspire to Plato's transcendent principles because they lacked the faculty of reason. He incorporated Platonic thought into Christian teachings, asserting that because humankind was created in God's image, we were closer to the divine than other forms of life. Like Plato and Aristotle, Augustine insisted that, because of their superior intellect and gift for rational thought, men had a direct link to the Christian God—a link that was not accorded to animals or women.

Nearly a thousand years later, Italian theologian St. Thomas Aquinas (1225–1274 CE) continued the synthesis of Greek philosophy and Christian doctrine begun by Augustine. Aquinas's extensive writings incorporated Aristotle's metaphysical conception of the Great Chain of Being into the Christian canon, placing God, Jesus Christ, angels, and saints above ordinary people on this hierarchical ladder. Animals and all other living things were positioned below humankind, further from the divine and God's grace.

Aquinas also refined the concept of the soul that medieval thinkers had inherited from the Greeks. The Greeks believed that the soul, which they called *pneuma* or breath, was the animating force in all life-forms. But Aquinas refined this notion, asserting that only people possessed a rational soul. The key word here is *rational*. Aquinas did not entirely deny that animals possessed souls, but he described their souls as *sentient*, meaning that an animal's soul is concerned only with sensory feelings and bodily sensations. Animals, or "dumb beasts," as they are sometimes referred to in the Bible, were believed to be motivated solely by base instincts and were completely lacking not only in the faculty of reason but even in self-awareness. Because animals cannot reasonably account for their actions before God, they cannot achieve salvation for their sins and gain entrance into heaven. Human beings, on the other hand, were believed to be self-aware and rational, giving us the ability to achieve salvation and enjoy eternal life.

Although notions about salvation have changed in contemporary Christian circles—focusing more on God's grace than on a rational accounting of one's actions—the idea that animals lacked rational souls and were therefore lesser beings than humans has long dominated Christian doctrine. Moreover, because Aquinas considered animals inferior to us, he did not believe we owed them any moral consideration whatsoever. "By the divine providence [animals] are intended for man's use in the natural order," he wrote. "Hence, it is not wrong for man to make use of them, either by killing or in any other way whatever."[2] This perspective rests in part on Aristotelian metaphysics, but it also rests on popular interpretations of a single word in a single passage in the Bible. That word is *dominion*.

## The Dominion Mandate

The hierarchical conception of the world that Christianity adopted from the ancient Greeks is evident in the origin story of the Bible's first book of Genesis. After creating the heavens and the earth—including the sun, moon, stars, plants, birds, water creatures, and animals—God then created humans:

> 26 And God said, Let us make man in our image, after our likeness: and let them have dominion over the fish of the sea, and over the fowl of the air, and over the cattle, and over all the earth, and over every creeping thing that creepeth upon the earth.
> 27 So God created man in his own image, in the image of God created him; male and female created He them.
> 28 And God blessed them, and God said unto them, Be fruitful, and multiply, and replenish the earth, and subdue it: and have dominion over the fish of the sea, and over the fowl of the air, and over every living thing that moveth upon the earth.

For two millennia, a debate has been raging in the Western world about the interpretation of the word *dominion* in Genesis 1:26 and 1:28. On one side of this debate, dominion is interpreted to mean that God granted humankind the right to rule over all living things on the earth and in the seas. This interpretation holds that human beings were created in the image of God and are therefore closer to God than other life-forms. Given our superior status, we can use animals as we see fit to meet our needs, including for labor, food, clothing, other materials, and entertainment. On the other side of this debate, the word *dominion* is interpreted to mean that, although God gave human beings control over animals and creation, we must exercise that control responsibly—a position referred to as "stewardship." The word *stewardship* doesn't appear in the Bible, but Christians who ascribe to this interpretation assert that caring for animals and the earth are deeply spiritual acts, and they take the responsibility of compassionate stewardship of God's creation very seriously.

Historically, the former perspective, which is sometimes called the *dominion mandate,* has dominated the Christian faith.[3] The Genesis passage quoted above is from the King James Version (KJV) of the Bible, one of the oldest English translations of biblical texts originally written in Hebrew and later translated into Latin by early Roman Catholic theologians such as Aquinas. Originally published in 1611, the KJV was generally accepted as the standard version of the Bible in the English-speaking Western world from the mid-seventeenth to the early twentieth centuries. Notably, in later versions of the Bible, the word *dominion* was changed to *rule*, reifying a hierarchical relationship between humankind and the rest of creation. This includes the New International Version (NIV) of the Bible, which was published in 1978 and is one of the most widely used in English-speaking Western countries.

Today, the popularity of the dominion mandate varies across Christian denominations. In a summary of official statements from religious institutions compiled by the Humane Society of the United

States, conservative Christian denominations such as Southern Baptist, Pentecostal, and the Church of Christ adhered most strongly to anthropocentric interpretations of biblical teachings about the cosmos.[4] These denominations generally encourage their followers to observe some limitations on their use of the earth's resources but fail to offer any specific information on what those limitations might entail. A good example is the statement issued by the Assemblies of God, the world's largest Pentecostal denomination, which states that "we feel Christians must act responsibly in their use of God's earth as we rightly harvest its resources. As stated in Genesis 1:27–30, we believe God has given mankind alone complete dominion (authority) over the earth's resources."[5]

Notably, studies have shown that the more religious a person is, the more likely they are to have an exploitive or utilitarian attitude toward animals.[6] They demonstrate that religion can have a profound impact on an individual's beliefs about animals and humankind's ethical obligation to them. They also show that Christianity as a religious institution is deeply anthropocentric.[7] While Christian leaders might encourage their congregants to treat animals with kindness and compassion, in practice this directive is often interpreted in an anthropocentric way, essentially giving people the right to use animals however they see fit to advance their interests. As noted by animal ethicist Paul Waldau, "The mainline Christian tradition [claims] that humans are so superior to the rest of creation that humans' morality rightfully excludes other animals' interests when they are in conflict with even minor human interests."[8] Some scholars go even further in their criticism of Christianity's anthropocentric perspective. In a journal article titled "The Historical Roots of Our Ecologic Crisis," historian Lynn White, Jr., writes, "Especially in its Western form, Christianity is the most anthropocentric religion the world has seen."[9] And in the book *Dominion: The Power of Man, the Suffering of Animals, and the Call to Mercy*, Andrew Scully writes, "Too often, too casually, we assume our interests always come first, and if it's profitable or expedient that is all we need to know. We assume that all these other creatures with whom we share the earth are here for us, and only for us. We assume, in effect, that we are everything and they are nothing."[10]

Whatever your personal beliefs about this topic, it's undeniable that the dominion mandate has had a profound influence on the way animals are viewed and treated in our society. Christianity is the world's dominant religion and has played a major role in shaping Western society's values and behavioral norms. Even people who are not religious, including those who identify as atheist, have been deeply influenced by Christianity simply because Western culture has embraced Christian ideas for nearly two thousand years.

That said, our religious institutions are not as powerful as they once were. In the twentieth century, scientific perspectives about the cosmos and the natural world began to challenge the absolute allegiance to the Christian worldview that had long characterized Western civilization. Today, most people think of religion and science as polar opposites. Yet this is not entirely the case. Both camps have long embraced the idea that animals can be used to serve human wants and needs.

## Cartesian Dualism

Western Europe's Scientific Revolution began around 1500, about three hundred years after St. Thomas Aquinas codified the hierarchical conception of the world as represented by Aristotle's Great Chain of Being into Christian doctrine. It was a heady time in Western Europe. Human beings were demonstrating a remarkable ability to understand and control their environment, and scientific inquiry was becoming increasingly widespread, especially among wealthy, well-educated men. One of the most influential thinkers of that time was French philosopher and scientist René Descartes (1596–1650 CE). Descartes was a quintessential representative of his well-educated class: a mathematician who connected the previously separate fields of geometry and algebra into analytic geometry; a philosopher who carried on the

Greek tradition of contemplating the nature of humankind, the natural world, and the cosmos; and a scientist who studied the natural world and sought to unlock its secrets.

The challenge for Descartes and his fellow scientist-philosophers was to incorporate new scientific understandings of the physical world into the Christian worldview, which held that God was perfect and all-powerful and the earth was the center of the universe. These ideas were not open for debate. Scientists who defied foundational Christian beliefs sometimes paid for their transgressions with their lives. In 1600 the Catholic Inquisition condemned philosopher and cosmologist Giordano Bruno for heresy and burned him alive for suggesting that the stars are suns surrounded by planetary worlds like our own.[11] Similarly, the Roman Catholic Church condemned Italian physicist and astronomer Galileo Galilei in 1633 for insisting that the earth revolves around the sun. Galileo spent the rest of his life under house arrest, and it took more than three hundred years for the church to clear his name of heresy.[12]

Christianity may have been ascendant in medieval Europe, but ancient pagan beliefs in which the physical and spiritual worlds were inseparable were still widespread, especially among common folk who were highly superstitious. Although most commoners dutifully worshipped in the Christian churches that had sprung up everywhere in their communities, many continued to believe that spirits abounded in the natural world, especially in animals. The notion that people could transform into animals and vice versa was also widespread. The early Roman Catholic Church challenged these ancient beliefs with violence. Tens of thousands of people, almost all of them women, were burned as witches because of their heretical beliefs. Many who were persecuted were accused of being possessed by evil demons and animal spirits, and those who had close relationships with animals, known as familiars, were particularly suspect.

It was in this religiously charged world that Descartes undertook his studies of the natural world. Deeply curious about physiology and anatomy, he regularly dissected human cadavers to study the circulatory system and internal organs. He also engaged in the controversial practice of vivisection, which is the dissection of live animals without anesthesia. It was Descartes who famously coined the phrase *bête machine*, which literally translates as "animal machine." He maintained that animals have no minds or souls (the terms were synonymous at that time) and are therefore complex machines, like watches. He also reasoned that, because animals are merely mindless and soulless machines, they don't experience pain.

Fascinated by the complexity of human and animal physiology, Descartes entertained a highly mechanistic view of the living world. In an essay titled *Treatise of Man*, Descartes wrote that "every life phenomenon represented a mechanical process exclusively," and "there is no reason to assume the existence of a 'feeling soul' or any factor of life and motion, except blood and breath which are moved by the heat of the fire that is continuously burning in the heart."[13] These were radical, blasphemous ideas that challenged the doctrine of the immortal human soul, and the Roman Catholic Church was not pleased. According to scholar Dénes Karasszon in *A Concise History of Veterinary Medicine*, "Although Descartes never attacked religion, his writings were put on the Index of the Vatican" (not a list you want your name on), and the French crown banned announcement of his ideas.[14]

Yet the historical record also indicates that Descartes was deeply devoted to the church. Descartes biographer Stephen Gaukroger writes that Descartes was a "zealous Roman Catholic who feared the displeasure of the Church above all else."[15] He purportedly stayed the publication of a book he'd been working on that supported Galileo's contention that the sun was the center of the universe, and he even burned part of the manuscript.[16] In his studies, Descartes sought to make his observations about the natural world compatible with Christian doctrine, and in 1641 he published a book titled *Meditations in First Philosophy* in which he formulated a philosophical framework that posited that the human soul was transcendent and distinct from the physical body.

Descartes ultimately identified an organ in the middle of the human brain where he claimed the elements of the mind or soul, believed to be placed there by God, met and interacted with the body. We've since learned that the organ Descartes identified as the "seat of the soul" is the pineal gland, whose actual function is to produce melatonin.[17] Nearly all vertebrate animals—including the dogs Descartes dissected—have pineal glands. But Descartes apparently overlooked or possibly denied this fact out of fear of the church, zealous religiosity, ambition, or a combination of these motivations.

Descartes's metaphysical perspective eventually came to be known as *Cartesian dualism*, which holds that the soul is a unique substance that exists separately from the body. Cartesian dualism marked a fundamental shift in the way Westerners thought about and interacted with animals and the natural world. In earlier centuries, when paganism was widespread, the natural world was suffused with spirits, and animals were often considered to be messengers of the gods. But following Europe's Scientific Revolution, this perspective was systematically suppressed by the emerging scientific community and the Christian church.

The profound impact of this paradigm shift on the Western mind is difficult to appreciate, in part because Cartesian dualism remains largely unchallenged. Most Westerners continue to believe that our souls are distinct and separate from our bodies. Yet many thinkers have pointed out the negative repercussions of this seemingly innocuous idea. In *The Death of Nature: Women, Ecology, and the Scientific Revolution*, ecofeminist and historian Carolyn Merchant explores the impact of Descartes's work and other influential figures of the Scientific Revolution on the relationship between humans and the natural world.[18] She makes a compelling case that after the revolution, the dominant Western perspective about the natural world veered strongly toward the belief that nature is a machine that we can and should control. When this shift occurred, we began to see animals and the earth itself as objects—useful tools without feelings or rights—rather than complex, living beings with whom we're deeply connected. Indeed, Buddhist priest Eshin Nishimura asserts that when Cartesian dualism was embraced in the West, "humans became a solitary island floating in the dead ocean of 'things.'"[19]

In the centuries that followed the introduction of Cartesian dualism in the sixteenth century, Western civilization flourished and spread around the globe. Animals played a key role in this growth, especially in the years leading up to the eighteenth century's Industrial Revolution, when we depended heavily on animals for labor in agriculture and the transport of goods, not to mention meat and other materials such as skins and textiles. The commodification of animals of all species, including those we keep as companions, continues to this day throughout the world.

## A Controversial but Enduring Paradigm

The foundational ideas reviewed in this chapter were not without their detractors, neither historically or today. There have always been people who questioned Platonic ideas about perfect forms and the divine quality of reason; the strict hierarchy of Aristotle's Great Chain of Being; the Christian notion of a dominion mandate; and Cartesian dualism. There have also been countless people who valued animals and the unique gifts they bring to this world, and who believed we have a moral obligation to treat them with respect and compassion. As noted by political philosopher and historian Rod Preece, "Although Western culture, in its subservience to commercial, industrial and technological innovation, has scarcely been what is commonly called 'at one with nature,' a concern with the status of our fellow animal relatives has never been entirely absent from Western consciousness."[20]

In the classic Greek era, for example, some philosophers challenged the hierarchical view of the world represented by Aristotle's

Great Chain of Being. Plutarch observed that "animals possessed intelligence, probity, ardour, and courage, and . . . their lives were in many respects superior to those of humans."[21] Christian mystics, who flourished in Western Europe in the Middle Ages, believed we have a moral obligation to care for our fellow creatures and the natural world with the same kindness and compassion that God calls on us to bestow on each other. Many Christian saints practiced compassion for creation throughout their lives, such as St. Francis of Assisi, a twelfth-century Catholic priest who considered all of nature to be the mirror of God and has long been celebrated as the patron saint of animals. In scientific circles, Descartes's contemporaries and the philosophers and scientists who followed in his footsteps decried the cruelty of vivisection. In 1764, French philosopher Voltaire wrote of Descartes, "You discover in [animals] all the same organs of feeling as in yourself. Answer me, mechanist, has Nature arranged all the springs of feeling in this animal to the end that he might not feel?"[22]

Despite the efforts of countless people to promote an animal- and earth-friendly worldview, the core ideas described in this chapter have endured and shaped our lives and the lives of animals in countless ways. Ideas can be tenacious. While the Western world has changed dramatically over the last two millennia, it's astonishing to consider how much has stayed the same. Entrenched vestiges of our culture's bias against animals are everywhere in our world. It was on full display in my family of origin when my dad catnapped Cricket and her two kittens, and it's also evident in many other aspects of our daily lives. In the next chapter, we'll begin our exploration of how the foundational ideas discussed in this chapter have impacted people and animals in the modern world.

C H A P T E R  4

# Discussion Questions

1. One of the core ideas discussed in the chapter is Plato's belief that reason or rational thinking is divine and an exclusively human quality. Do you agree with this perspective? And how do you think this idea has impacted our relationship with other animals? Provide examples to support your answer.

2. How do you interpret the word *dominion* in the first book of Genesis in the Bible?

3. How do you believe Christianity's dominion mandate has impacted the way we think about and interact with animals in Western society? Provide examples to support your answer.

4. One of the core ideas described in this chapter is Cartesian dualism, or the belief that the physical and spiritual are distinct and separate entities. Do you agree with this idea? Why or why not?

5. What impact do you believe Cartesian dualism has had on the way we think about and interact with animals? Provide examples to support your answer.

# The Hidden Challenges
of Pet Keeping

## CHAPTER 5

# Almost Family Members

In 2004 I was invited to serve as the on-call chaplain at the veterinary teaching hospital at North Carolina State University (NCSU). I wore a badge that read "chaplain," and carried a twenty-four-hour pager. I stopped by the hospital for a few hours every day, including on weekends. Just as I'd done rounds at my local hospital, I did rounds at the veterinary hospital, circling through the small and large animal clinics, waiting rooms, intensive care department, and emergency room. I spoke with pet keepers about their ill or deceased animals. I attended euthanasia procedures in the "quiet rooms" of the small animal hospital and in the fields behind the large animal hospital. I dropped in on Christmas Eve and prayed for the animals and clinical staff in the intensive care unit. I also spoke with faculty, staff, and students, especially when they had a difficult case.

I left my position at NCSU's veterinary teaching hospital in late 2006. Not long afterward, I had lunch with a work colleague who was a clinical counselor. We talked about my work at the hospital, and I remember casually mentioning that some of the pet keepers I'd met grieved intensely when they lost their animals. In response, my colleague remarked that people who grieve intensely for animals have an "irrational attachment" to them. I was puzzled and alarmed by her response, and I wondered how this woman would approach grieving pet keepers if she encountered them in her counseling work. In my experience, many pet keepers can easily be labeled as "irrationally attached" to their animals, although I dislike the term and believe it wrongly paints people who have strong attachments to animals as psychologically dysfunctional. Most pet keepers consider their pets family members, deserving of the same care and respect as their human family members. Yet a closer look at pet keeping in the modern West reveals that our society does not consistently honor this perspective.

This chapter is the first of three that will explore how our society's anthropocentric paradigm and the core ideas that drive this human-first worldview play out in our lives and the lives of our animal friends. This discussion will focus on three areas of concern: perspectives about animals and the human-animal bond in the field of psychology and other social sciences; the legal status of animals as property; and the pet industry. There are undoubtedly many other challenges related to anthropocentrism that warrant discussion, but I've chosen those that I feel are most relevant to the pet-keeping community.

## Pets as Ersatz People

When my colleague said that people who grieve intensely for their animals have an "irrational attachment," she may have been reflecting the quality of her education. The field of psychology—like other humanities disciplines, such as anthropology, sociology, and philosophy—has long assumed that animals are inferior to humans, and training for clinical counselors reflects this assumption.

Beginning in the 1950s, psychologists, anthropologists, and other scholars began studying the human impulse to keep pets and the psychological and practical value of pet keeping. They also sought to identify the psychological differences between people who keep pets and those who don't. A common theme eventually emerged from these studies and became a dominant narrative in the humanities. This perspective holds that pets are second-rate substitutes for people who can't maintain satisfying human relationships, and people with especially strong attachments to pets are believed to be psychologically flawed. In the book *In the Company of Animals*, professor of animal ethics and welfare James Serpell refers to this idea as the "ersatz relationship theory."[1] He asserts that critics of pet keeping "appear to believe that pet owners are somehow socially inadequate and that they use their pets in much the same way that drug users use heroin, as artificial and ultimately detrimental substitutes for reality."[2] Other scholars have positioned pets as parasites who take advantage of their human hosts, an idea promoted by British psychologist John Archer in a 2011 article titled "Pet Keeping: A Case Study in Maladaptive Behavior."[3] Among the "maladaptive behaviors" that Archer explores is the inclination of pet keepers to regard attachments to pets more favorably than their attachment to humans.

Granted, there are people who struggle to find satisfying relationships with other people but who connect well with animals, such as the autistic child who responds only to a therapy dog. It's also true that mental illness is sometimes expressed through pets. Serpell describes the case of a California woman who seemed unconcerned when her dog ate her infant.[4] Pet hoarding is also very troubling, like the two hundred malnourished and sick animals who were removed from a small single-family home in the Boston area in 2014.[5] Sensational stories like these get a lot of press, further entrenching the idea that there's something psychologically wrong with people who have strong attachments to animals. But such cases are rare and represent the extremes of pet keeping. They're also indicative of neurotic behavior that happens to focus on pets, and they don't reflect the behavior of most pet keepers.

The bottom line is that the "ersatz relationship theory" doesn't hold up to scrutiny. A US study found "no significant correlation between attachment to a pet and either avoidance or anxiety" in pet keepers' relationships with other people.[6] Similarly, in his exhaustive exploration of academic research on the topic, Serpell concludes that "we have no good evidence that the majority of pet-owners are any different from anyone else, or that they use their pets as ersatz replacements for people."[7] My experience working with grieving pet keepers supports this conclusion. I've met many people who rely on their pets for companionship and love but also have very satisfying human relationships. I also think it's important to acknowledge that pets make better company than many people do when it comes to the qualities we value in our closest relationships, such as trustworthiness, loyalty, and nonjudgmental love.

In the final analysis, it's reasonable to conclude that scholars who promote the "ersatz relationship theory" are operating from a cultural bias that assumes relationships with pets are inherently inferior to relationships with people. This bias has had a knock-on effect on the field of clinical counseling. Currently, educational programs for clinical counselors and therapists don't include training specific to pet keeping and loss. A qualitative study of pet loss counselors in the UK found that counselors must seek postgraduate training and that, among their counseling peers, therapy for pet loss is not considered "real counselling" and "lacks in perceived importance in counselling training and practice."[8] A US study comparing the loss of human loved ones with the loss of pets found that pet keepers are often reluctant to seek professional help for their grief from clinical counselors out of fear that their feelings won't be taken seriously.[9] The study's authors write that their research "draws attention to the need for professionals such as counselors and therapists to develop greater self-awareness and acceptance around responding to individuals who have experienced the death of a companion animal. By identifying the grief process as normative and comparable to that of a human death, professionals can create a supportive environment that promotes understanding, validation and long-term well-being."[10]

On a positive note, there are signs that the prevailing view of animals among psychologists is shifting. The website Psychology Today includes many articles and blog posts that explore the benefits of pet keeping, acknowledge the difficulty of pet loss, and generally offer a positive perspective on animal companions and their importance to us. Training in pet loss for clinical counselors and social workers is expanding, primarily through online continuing education or certification courses. These developments are a direct response to the growing popularity of pet keeping in the West. Indeed, pet keeping has become so widespread that psychologists and other caregivers can no longer easily characterize pet keepers as "irrationally attached" to their animals. I'm hopeful that this trend will continue as more pet keepers ask for the support they need.

## Animals as Property

In theory, a society's legal system should reflect its values, so an examination of laws can reveal a great deal about what's important to us and what isn't. Currently, animals are legally considered property throughout the world, and this designation limits their legal rights.

Although most pet keepers consider their animals to be valued members of their families, pets are nonetheless legally equivalent to inanimate objects or commodities. Attorney Patricia Fersch captures the absurdity of this legal arrangement when she asks: "Do we refer to our pets as property—a piece of furniture or a lamp? Do we sleep with our furniture or lamps or call them by name into bed at night? Do we take the sofa for a walk or groom it regularly and lovingly with special brushes and bath soaps? Do we name our furniture? Do we refer to ourselves as mommy or daddy about furniture?"[11]

In the US, full legal protection depends on the designation of *personhood*, which confers many privileges in court, including the ability to seek restitution for abuse, neglect, and other forms of harm. Ironically, corporations and ships are defined as persons for limited legal purposes in the US, but animals are not. If legal personhood were granted to animals, it would not confer all the legal rights enjoyed by people. Rather, personhood status would legally protect the interests of a particular animal. Granting personhood status to a dog, for example, would not give that dog the right to vote, but it might give them the right not to be used for scientific experimentation.

As it is, however, the legal status of pets and other animals as property limits their protections from cruelty and neglect. Pet keepers face limitations in their ability to seek justice for the abuse of an animal by a domestic partner or a disgruntled neighbor, and an animal who was adopted from a rescue is legally considered worthless. Similarly, pet keepers' ability to secure compensation for medical negligence by veterinarians is limited. I've met people whose world was turned upside down because a medical procedure did not go as planned, and their animal died unexpectedly. One woman told me she had no idea her animal's life was worthless in a court of law. It was simply unfathomable to her that the dog she loved so much could be of so little value in a society where pet keeping is so popular. There was nothing she could do to hold her veterinarian accountable for what she considered malpractice, and she was frustrated and disillusioned.

Euthanasia also raises some sticky legal issues. Veterinarians cannot legally make the decision to euthanize an animal or when to carry out the procedure. They can advise someone about their pet's medical condition and work with them to evaluate their quality of life, but only the pet keeper has the legal authority to euthanize their animal. A tragic consequence of this legal framework is that people have the legal authority to refuse euthanasia, even when it is clearly in the best interest of animals who are suffering. Conversely, so-called convenience euthanasia, in which someone seeks to end the life of a healthy animal for frivolous reasons, places veterinarians in an ethical quandary. While most will refuse to euthanize a healthy animal, veterinarians also know it's possible that unwanted animals will be taken to a kill shelter, where they will likely be put to death, depending on their adoptability.

Despite these challenges, some veterinarians are wary of granting personhood status to companion animals. If such laws were enacted, they argue, pet keepers could more easily sue veterinarians for punitive damages for mental anguish and loss of companionship, making veterinary insurance rates prohibitive. The practice of euthanasia itself could become problematic if animals had personhood status because the euthanasia of people, known as "medical aid in dying," is currently against the law in most states in the US and other Western countries.

Beyond laws that classify animals as property, animal welfare and anti-cruelty laws in the US and abroad offer limited legal protections. The main federal law in the US is the 1966 Animal Welfare Act (AWA). The AWA is concerned primarily with animals kept in zoos and used in laboratories, but dogs who are bred and sold in puppy mills are also protected under this legislation. The AWA requires that minimum standards be maintained for the handling, care, treatment, and transportation of animals. The AWA also prohibits dog fighting when the activity crosses state lines. However, animal advocates claim that the AWA is not well enforced, and inhumane practices often go unchecked at puppy mills and in other settings where animals are bred and sold.

Most welfare laws for companion animals in the US occur at the state level. Every state has laws governing animal care, though these laws vary widely from state to state.[12] The most common laws regulate how long animal shelters must hold stray animals before they can be adopted or euthanized; rabies vaccination for dogs and cats; and the commercial breeding of companion animals. Some states have also adopted hot-car laws that criminalize leaving an animal in a closed vehicle in extreme weather and anti-tethering laws that limit how long animals can be tied up outside, especially in extreme weather. In the US, some states have laws that allow pets to be included in domestic violence protective orders, and all states have laws that make it a felony to purposely kill a dog or a cat.

In recent years, some states have enacted laws requiring courts to consider an animal's best interests in custody disputes that arise when couples divorce. Currently, eight states consider a pet's well-being or best interest when determining joint or sole ownership in divorce cases. Attorney Patricia Fersch notes that litigating pet custody requires "proving that you were the primary care giver of the animal. This requires proof as to who fed the animal, who took the animal for walks, who groomed the animal such as brushing and bathing, who took the animal to his/her [veterinary] appointments, who socialized with the animal. If you're found to be the primary care provider, you're likely to obtain custody of the pet."[13]

Despite these developments, authorities can easily nullify legal protections for animals. In *Just a Dog: Understanding Animal Cruelty and Ourselves*, sociologist Arnold Arluke describes a courtroom scene in which some teenagers were on trial for beating a dog nearly to death:

> The judge summarily dismissed the egregious case of animal cruelty against [the dog], despite strong evidence that the dog was hideously beaten with baseball bats. People standing near the bench heard the judge glibly mumbling, "It's just a dog . . ." as he moved on to a "more important case," a liquor store "B & E." The humane law enforcement agents who prosecuted [the dog's] case felt a surge of anger and frustration, seeing their effort go nowhere. The abusers disappeared quickly from the courtroom, still puzzled about why such a 'big stink' was made over a dog.[14]

Progress in legal battles to protect animals from undue suffering and death has been incremental at best. Animals and people suffer because of this legal arrangement. When you lose a pet because of a legal system that fails to protect that animal, you're likely to experience a special kind of grief. Melissa M. Kelley, assistant professor of pastoral care and counseling at the Boston College Clough School of Theology and Ministry, refers to this grief as the "grief of injustice," which is "grief due in whole or in part to injustice. It is grief that is caused by unjust structures and/or by unjust actions or inactions of individuals, groups, and systems. It is grief that is not part of the 'natural order' of things. It is grief that did not need to happen. It is grief that was preventable."[15]

## The Pet Biz

Pets are big business. Indeed, spending on pets in the US and other pet-loving countries has increased steadily. In the two decades from 1998 to 2018, total annual spending on pets in the US skyrocketed from $23 billion to $90.5 billion, a 393 percent increase.[16] In 2024, spending on pets reached nearly $152 billion.[17]

Yet a critical look at the modern pet industry shows that the excesses of our pet craze come at a high cost to millions of animals caught up in this system. In *Run, Spot, Run: The Ethics of Keeping Pets*, animal ethicist Jessica Pierce raises some compelling concerns about pet keeping in the US, citing issues with puppy and kitten mills, wholesale markets for exotic animals, high mortality rates in the pet shop industry, high levels of animal abuse and neglect, and the fact that a quarter of all companion animals lack basic veterinary care.[18] She describes these issues as the "dark undercurrents" of modern pet keeping and calls on pet keepers to take note of these trends. "Notwithstanding claims about humanization and bonding, large numbers of pets aren't getting any love or are getting the wrong kind," Pierce writes. "These undercurrents challenge even the most thoughtful and responsible pet owner because it is often hard to know what we might be doing wrong or how our actions might or might not be harming the animals we cannot see beyond the curtains of our own windows."[19]

The number of animals "we cannot see" is vast. Millions of animals die prematurely in the pet industry and the exotic species trade. According to one US study, up to 72 percent of exotic animals die before they reach a store.[20] Most pet stores sell sick and injured animals, fail to provide proper veterinary care, keep animals in unsanitary conditions, and use inhumane methods to dispose of sick or unwanted animals. Unregulated backyard breeders are guilty of many of the same unethical practices, and they regularly euthanize unsalable animals.

In the US, millions of cats and dogs are also euthanized in city and county shelters. Many of these animals are disposed of in government-run landfills. To draw attention to this practice, photographer Mary Shannon Johnstone took a living dog from the county-run animal shelter in Raleigh, North Carolina, to a local landfill where the mountains of trash had been covered in grass. Each dog was given one afternoon of unchecked freedom at the landfill before being returned to their cage at the shelter. She published her photos in a book and website titled *Landfill Dogs* (landfilldogs.com), juxtaposing photos of the dogs looking decidedly unhappy in their shelter cages with photos of the same dogs running and leaping at the landfill and taking naps in the grass. Johnstone writes that she chose the landfill for her photos "because the county animal shelter falls under the same management as the landfill. This government structure reflects a societal value: homeless cats and dogs are just another waste stream."[21] Johnstone took pictures of thirty dogs, all of them pit bulls. All were eventually adopted, and Johnstone raised more than $14,000 for the county animal shelter.

The US pet industry has flourished because the demand for companion animals has grown steadily in recent decades. This growth is partly due to more people discovering the rewards of keeping pets. Yet the lucrative pet industry has also undoubtedly had a powerful influence on the growth in pet keeping. Since the 1970s, the US public has been bombarded by TV shows, movies, advertising, and pet-focused websites that have popularized the idea that the ideal American home must include at least one dog playing in the yard and a cat or two lounging in the sunny spot by the bay window. Research shows that the popularity of specific animal species or breeds can be traced directly to their starring role in movies, a trend known as the "dog movie star effect."[22] One US study found that unrealistic portrayals of certain dog breeds in movies compel people to seek out a pet of that breed.[23] For ten years after the 1963 release of *The Incredible Journey*, which starred a Labrador retriever, the number of Labs registered with the US Kennel Club increased almost fivefold.[24] Unfortunately, people are sometimes unprepared for the realities of pet keeping or know little about the temperament of high-maintenance animals who often appear in films and in advertising, such as border collies. This sometimes results in buyer's remorse, which can lead to poor outcomes for the animals.

What's missing from our daily media diet about animals is the acknowledgment that keeping pets, for all its rewards, can be messy, inconvenient, time-consuming, and expensive. Many people don't understand the complex creatures they bring into their homes and are unprepared for the hard work and sacrifices required to properly care for them. A *Forbes Advisor* survey explored the perspectives of people who had acquired a dog and found that 54 percent had regrets. More than a quarter said they objected to cleaning up after their dog, while others cited difficulties caring for their dog when traveling or going to work. A similar proportion lacked the time and money required to properly train or socialize their dog; objected to the considerable cost of feeding their animal, including food and veterinary care; and struggled with irritating barking and whining.[25] No single issue made these new dog keepers regret their decision—it was the whole expensive, messy, noisy package. In response to these trends, animal rescue organizations devote considerable time and resources to educating people about animal behavior and the costs of keeping a pet.

While many animals benefit from our love, many others pay a high price for our pet obsession. People suffer as well. Veterinary workers grapple with anger, despair, and frustration when a client decides not to treat their sick animal even when they can afford to do so, or when someone asks to euthanize a healthy animal for frivolous and self-serving reasons. Workers in America's animal rescue and shelter system suffer because of the high numbers of unwanted animals and the ongoing need to control these populations through euthanasia. The statistics are troubling. Rates of depression, compassion fatigue, and suicide are above average in these groups, particularly among people who work in animal shelters.[26] Yet these challenges fly under the radar for most people, including pet keepers. I'll explore this topic in detail and discuss how spiritual caregivers can make a positive impact on the lives of animal care workers in *Veterinary Chaplaincy,* the next book in the Pet Chaplain Learning Series.

· · ·

The impact of our society's anti-animal bias on pets and pet keepers is often hidden from view. But then one day something unforeseen happens that shakes up your world, and you realize that your furry, feathered, or scaled family member is not quite the family member you thought they were, at least as far as Western society is concerned. Perhaps you've personally experienced some of the challenges described in this chapter. Maybe you encountered a counselor or therapist who questioned or minimized the intensity of your attachment to your pet and the grief you felt when you lost them. Or maybe you lost a pet due to medical malpractice and were forced to confront the limitations of a legal system that places no value on their life. You might also have discovered the harsh reality that pets acquired at a pet shop or from an unscrupulous breeder often have lifelong health problems.

For most people, the realization that losing a pet presents some unique challenges occurs when they discover that the family and friends they thought they could count on for support aren't as consistently supportive as they had hoped. Formal grief support resources, such as pet loss support groups, are also limited. In the next chapter, we'll continue our exploration of the impacts of anthropocentrism on our lives with a critical look at the social experiences surrounding pet keeping and loss in the modern West.

## CHAPTER 6

# The Lonely Journey of Pet Loss

The moment you realize you're alone in the world—that the people you count on the most don't really understand you—is one you never forget.

For a young woman named Anna, that moment came when she was about twelve years old. Anna and her two younger sisters were staying with her grandparents on the family farm. They were sleeping on the couch in the living room, and one morning, when her grandmother opened the door to let in the sunlight, Anna's world changed forever.

Her grandmother calmly told her that someone had run over her dog. Alarmed, Anna jumped off the couch and ran out to the street in front of the house. When I spoke with her, she recalled the bloody details of the scene:

> I went to the street and saw how bad it was. Cocoa's tail was all the way over on one side of the street, and her body was on the other, and it was all torn up. I mean, it was bad. And then my little sisters came out and saw me crying, and they made fun of me. They picked on me because they were young, and they didn't understand why I was crying over this dog.

And then my aunt came out and saw me crying, and she was like, "Why are you crying?" And I was like, "Well, I'm crying because my dog died and also crying because they're picking on me because my dog died." And she said, "You don't have to be so sad." She was trying to console me, but it didn't really work. I was crying about Cocoa, and I was crying because I was embarrassed about crying and because it just felt like I shouldn't cry over an animal. I think my aunt knew how hurt I was. She understood that I was hurt. But it was like I shouldn't be so hurt about it, like it was wrong to feel that way.

Anna shared this story with me when I interviewed her for my doctoral research study of pet keeping and loss. Although it had been many years since she lost Cocoa, her memories of that loss have stayed with her. So, too, has the alienation she experienced from her family when no one really understood her sadness about Cocoa. That event changed the way Anna expresses—or doesn't express—her feelings about animals.

"I felt hurt when Cocoa died," Anna said. "It felt like I couldn't come to my family when I was hurting, not only about my feelings toward a certain animal, but for anything I feel hurt about. I felt betrayed. That's why I shy away from expressing my feelings about my animals with other people. After Cocoa, with other animals I lost, I masked my feelings. I didn't let others see how I felt because I didn't want to get hurt all over again. I've never stopped feeling connected with animals, but I keep quiet about it."

Anna's story offers a stark example of the social alienation that is distressingly common among people who grieve intensely for their lost pets. When your feelings of sorrow are not recognized and validated by others—or if you don't share your feelings at all for fear of rejection or ridicule—the effects can be painful and long-lasting.

We have a saying in my pet loss support group: sympathy for the loss of a pet lasts for about three weeks, but the grief lasts much longer.

When you've lost a pet, your family and friends may be supportive at first but grow frustrated and anxious if your grief is intense or lasts a long time. Yet losing a pet can be as difficult, if not more difficult, than losing a human loved one. When others don't understand or honor your grief, your relationships with the people you're closest to can become strained, and your grief more difficult to manage.

Of all the ways that anthropocentrism plays out in our daily lives, social disenfranchisement is the most deeply personal. Being rejected or ridiculed for how you feel not only wounds your heart, or the sense that you're loved. It also wounds your spirit, or the sense that you belong.

Human beings are intensely social creatures. We crave acceptance and often go to great lengths to win the approval of others, especially those we interact with regularly. When the people in our lives value what we love, we generally feel that all is right with the world. We draw comfort from the knowledge that others feel as we do and value what we value. But when that's not the case, we might isolate ourselves and struggle with feelings of alienation.

Given our need for social acceptance, it's no surprise that animal people tend to surround themselves with other animal people. Some people grow up in animal-loving families and are surrounded by a reliable community of like-minded pet enthusiasts. Others purposely seek out people who share their passion and might withdraw from people who don't understand them. Yet it's impossible to entirely escape the social disenfranchisement that comes with loving creatures who are still viewed by many in our society as useful objects. Nearly every devoted pet keeper I've ever met has felt the sting of being called a "crazy cat lady" or an "animal nut" at some point in their life. Many wear these badges with pride, but their nonchalance reflects deeper wounds.

The term *disenfranchised* is unusual but accurate. When you have a franchise on something, you have something of value. When you're disenfranchised, you've lost something of value. When it comes to pets, the thing you've lost is social acknowledgment of your love for your pet and the grief you experienced when you lost them. At a cultural level, if not at a personal level, you're essentially being told that your loss doesn't matter and the pet you cherished isn't worth grieving.

In the pet-keeping world, we talk most often about disenfranchised grief. But people who love animals typically experience some degree of social isolation throughout their lives. In this chapter, I'll explore three related kinds of social disenfranchisement: disenfranchised love, disenfranchised grief, and self-disenfranchisement.

## Disenfranchised Love

While most American households keep one or more animals, millions don't keep pets. Some people are indifferent to animals, while others question or even ridicule the lengths to which some pet enthusiasts will go to pamper their animals. Lavish spending on pets is sometimes viewed as a betrayal of the human species, and some critics of pet keeping maintain that we could solve world hunger with all the money people in wealthy countries spend on their animal companions. Stereotypes abound of unhinged animal lovers. The trope of the eccentric woman who keeps pets because she can't have children of her own is common, as is the idea that the homes of pet keepers are always smelly and dirty.

Some people think animals are not worth the time, energy, and expense that pet keeping requires. One online opinion writer bemoaned the fact that, as someone who dislikes dogs, she feels ostracized in a dog-loving culture. "I was—and am—in a state of my life in which I would rather interact with real humans than play fetch with furry neighbors at the dog park," Tatiana Gallardo wrote. "The thought of having to care for a creature that can't even hold a conversation with me is not enticing. It is a colossal waste of my money and energy. This is where I feel like I need to make a promise: I swear I am not a cold-hearted freak. I just have different priorities than dog-lovers do.

I think dogs are smelly, unclean, annoying, and, ultimately, too much work. I shouldn't have to apologize for this."[1]

Given the negative way some people in our society view animals, people who are passionate about their fellow creatures will not always see eye to eye with family members, friends, and others in their social circles. Some may be reluctant to reveal the intensity of their attachment to their pets unless they know that the person they're speaking with shares their passion. In *Pack of Two*, author Caroline Knapp describes falling in love with her dog Lucy and realizing that her friends didn't entirely understand the transformation they saw in her. "Dog lovers feel like members of a secret society, as though we're inhabiting a strange and somehow improper universe," Knapp wrote. "Unless you fall back on the one or two pat explanations we routinely trot out in order to explain the canine place in the human heart—dogs give us unconditional love, dogs are 'good companions'—it's hard to talk about loving a dog deeply without inviting skepticism. A lot of people, quite frankly, think intense attachments to animals are weird and suspect, the domain of people who can't quite handle attachments to humans."[2]

About a quarter of the vet tech students I interviewed felt like outliers in their social circles, and their feelings of alienation began long before their pet was lost. Rachel told me that, even though her childhood family always had a dog or two in the house, her parents weren't "pet people." She also said that "for some people, getting animals is almost like collecting. It's not really about the animal at all. It's as if the animal is an accessory, like a colored watch band or a handbag. For some people, it's not necessarily an attachment to the animal they have; it's more the idea of, 'I have a dog that looks vicious, or I have a dog that looks like a little stuffed animal.' I've grown up with family members who are like that. . . . It was hurtful because I thought about animals differently than they did."

People in farming communities who are passionate about animals sometimes struggle to find social acceptance. In the rural US, animals are widely regarded in utilitarian ways, a perspective that is rooted in our agrarian past. Animals are also often tightly categorized in rural communities. A farm family might keep a house dog who lives mostly indoors and others who are strictly working dogs (hunting partners, herders, or guards) and spend most of their lives outside. Barn cats are kept to control rodents, as they have been for thousands of years. Horses are generally kept for pleasure riding and for competition, such as rodeoing. Most other farm animals—cows, chickens, turkeys, pigs, goats, and sheep—are raised solely for their meat or material.

Many farm families take good care of their animals because their livelihood depends on them. Yet most of these animals are still considered commodities and are treated as such, so the care they receive ultimately flows from a profit motive rather than from emotional attachment. In the US, 4-H programs play an important role in perpetuating the dominant view that some animals are, first and foremost, property or chattel. Children as young as six or seven who compete in 4-H events sometimes become emotionally attached to the animals in their care and struggle when they must relinquish them or witness them being taken away for slaughter. Parents, teachers, and 4-H leaders encourage children to maintain emotional distance from their animals, for example, by not naming the animals they raise. Eventually, most children appear to accept their animals' fate as necessary and proper and learn to keep their emotions in check.

Not all children fare well in this environment. Many people who grew up on farms have told me that they grieved when the animals they were close to as children were killed without remorse. Five of the vet tech students I interviewed grew up on farms. One particularly gut-wrenching story was shared by a young woman named Helen, who kept pigs as pets. When her family's large-animal veterinarian botched the castration of Wilbur, her pet potbelly pig, Helen was horrified and angry. When she confronted the vet about his culpability in Wilbur's death, he responded by saying that Wilbur was "just a pig. I'll get you another one." Helen was incensed. "I'm a client of yours, and you pretty much killed my pet," she told him. "Yeah, he's just a pig to you, but not to me. He was my baby."

Another student, Mollie, struggled to find understanding and acceptance in her family and small farming community, where animals were considered useful tools or a source of food. Mollie reluctantly accepted this perspective. "That's the way it is on a farm," she said. "My dad calls it 'the way of life.' The way of life is that animals live, animals die. We don't like it. We're never going to like losing someone we care about. But it's hard sometimes. I've always had a hard time when my animals died." She told a story about a club-footed calf she had helped birth. Her uncle wanted to kill the calf because his malformation made him useless, but Mollie was adamant that his life was worth saving. She was just a kid at the time, but she dedicated all her spare time to caring for the calf, which meant getting up before dawn and tending to him again when she got home from school and before she went to bed. The calf survived and eventually became one of the biggest cows in the family's herd.

When her horse Honey died, Mollie was devastated, and she struggled to find support among her family and friends. "They couldn't really understand why I was so upset," Mollie said. "My best friend rides horses and took riding lessons and all. But she didn't grow up with the passion for animals that I have. She likes them, and she loves them, but there's no passion. And because I have such a passion for them, it hurts me so much more."

## Disenfranchised Grief

The phrase *disenfranchised grief* was coined in 1989 by Lutheran minister, professor, and grief expert Dr. Kenneth Doka to describe the grief experienced for any loss that is not socially recognized.[3] In the US, people sometimes experience disenfranchised grief when they lose a same-sex partner or suffer a miscarriage or infertility; lose a family member or friend to suicide; go through a divorce or lose a job; or lose mobility and independence due to illness or aging. In person-pet relationships, disenfranchised grief occurs because pets are considered inferior to people and are therefore considered less worthy of our sorrow when they're lost.

The death of a pet is still often trivialized in our society, and you might feel that you should be able to weather the loss of your animal friends with relative ease. When speaking with casual acquaintances or coworkers, you might receive a few polite words of condolence or the advice that getting a new pet will make you feel better. But if you share the fact that losing your pet was more painful than losing your mother (or brother or friend and so on), you might be met with a skeptical silence or possibly shock and indignation that you could possibly grieve more for an animal than a person.

Pet keepers know instinctively or learn very quickly that they must be careful who they talk to about their feelings. Many suffer alone. One study found that nearly 75 percent of American pet keepers grieve privately after the loss of their pet.[4] Other studies have reported that people distance themselves from others and become socially isolated when their pet dies.[5] In a qualitative study of people who'd recently euthanized their animal, many said they were afraid to share their grief with their family and friends because they didn't think anyone would understand their feelings.[6] In contrast, when we lose a human loved one, most of us can rely on the support of our communities, and such support is strongly associated with what is described as a "positive grieving experience."[7]

When others fail to acknowledge or honor your sorrow, when they urge you to "move on" after a few weeks or, worse, remind you that your pet was "just an animal," your grief journey is likely to be more difficult. Disenfranchisement—and the social isolation it brings—is the salt in the wound of pet loss. Such alienation can shape your life in profound ways. You might grow distant from those who failed to honor your grief and, in doing so, failed to honor your love. You might hide your pain or deny your feelings altogether. Or you might strike out, angry at the betrayal and determined to make your pain known.

Social disenfranchisement can also have adverse effects on your physical health. Neurological studies using advanced imaging technology have shown that social exclusion activates the same areas of the brain as physical injury.[8] If you don't talk about your grief, you risk internalizing these powerful emotions, which can lead to depression, poor physical health, and increased stress.[9] The equation is simple: if others minimize or dismiss your grief or, worse, think that your attachment to your pet is irrational, then you're likely to feel even more miserable than you already do and for a longer period of time.

The flip side of disenfranchised grief might be called *enfranchised grief*. If you're lucky, your family and friends will rally around you and support you as best they can. You might even have a family member who is very attached to your pet, and you can rely on each other. It's incredibly comforting when you have the freedom to share your feelings honestly with others, without worrying that you'll be misunderstood or told that you're overreacting. When other people acknowledge your pain and respond consistently with genuine sympathy, you're likely to feel better sooner than you otherwise would.

The high costs of disenfranchised grief—and the wonderful benefits of sympathetic support—were an important finding in my research study with the vet tech students. Many of the students came from pet-friendly homes and communities and were supported by friends, family, coworkers, and others in their social sphere. After losing his cat Muppet, Frank relied on his mother for support, and he also found support in a tight-knit community of animal-loving friends and coworkers. Muppet was buried at an informal pet cemetery maintained by one of Frank's former work supervisors. Though he missed her terribly, Frank said he never received any responses he considered unsupportive or inappropriate, such as the suggestion that he get another pet.

But almost half the students I interviewed had social interactions after losing their pets that were unsupportive. A young woman named Lillian said she "shut down" emotionally when a friend questioned her intense grief for the loss of her cat, remarking that he was "just a cat." Another student, Celeste, said that she struggled to find support when her dog Rambo died. "Nobody really understood how I felt after Rambo died," she said. "There was nobody who would talk to me. I wasn't close to my mother, and she wasn't an animal person. My sisters would just say, 'Well, you'll get over it. Get another pet.' Or friends would say, 'Yeah, I'm sorry you're going through this, but you'll get over it.' And that's about all I heard. There was no consolation."

The point is that grief is not personal; it's *relational*. We often use the terms *grief, bereavement*, and *mourning* interchangeably. But there are subtle differences between them, and these differences offer valuable insight into the phenomenon of disenfranchised grief. To explicate these ideas, I'd like to turn to the work of social science researchers Kathy Charmaz and Melinda Milligan. In a chapter titled "Grief" in *The Handbook of the Sociology of Emotions*, Charmaz and Milligan offer the following definitions of these common terms.[10]

**Grief:** Grief is the subjective response to a painful or distressing event. When we speak of grief, we are referring to the personal emotions and physical sensations that typically accompany the loss of a loved one or some other distressing, life-changing event.

**Bereavement:** This term is often confused with grief, but it refers to a survivor's social status following public acknowledgment of a loss. Achieving bereavement status depends on the general expectation that the survivor will grieve. In Western society, we're expected to grieve deeply for some family members, such as spouses, children, parents, and siblings, but to grieve less for grandparents, aunts, uncles, cousins, and other members of our extended families. Yet bereavement status is conferred even in the absence of grief, like the widow who feels more relief than sadness at the death of her abusive husband. Conversely, not every grieving person is granted full bereavement status. People who've lost a pet may be expected to grieve but are not granted the same bereavement status afforded to those grieving the loss of a spouse, even though their grief may be equally, if not more, intense. Many people have told me that they were expected to grieve the loss of a distant relative whom they barely knew but were not permitted to grieve the loss of a pet they dearly loved.

**Mourning:** Mourning encompasses the culturally approved practices, rituals, and traditions that we engage in following death. Examples in Western society include dressing in black and conducting memorial services, funerals, and wakes. Such traditions exist on an institutional level, though people may create their own rituals. As with bereavement status, mourning rituals are sometimes observed in the absence of actual grief. Similarly, people may grieve without having reliable access to collective rituals of mourning. This includes most pet keepers. As we'll see in the next chapter, the death rituals we're accustomed to when we lose a human loved one are generally not available for pets. Yet public rituals are an important coping mechanism. They're the cultural signposts we can follow when we're lost in the disorienting chaos of despair. But achieving bereavement status and gaining acceptance into mourning rituals begin with the social acknowledgment of a loss. If others do not validate your grief, then you're not considered truly bereaved or in mourning. Your grief becomes socially invisible.

## Self-Disenfranchisement

It can be very distressing when you feel disenfranchised by others after losing a pet. But it's arguably worse when you disenfranchise yourself.

Many people minimize their feelings about their pets. A study that compared the loss of human loved ones with the loss of pets found that the grief people experienced was comparable in terms of intensity and duration. The study authors noted, however, that people who'd lost pets often avoided "seeking personal and professional support . . . thus self-imposing disenfranchised grief and internalizing societal norms around hierarchies of grief."[11] When the people in our lives and society as a whole tell us that a pet is "just an animal" and that we should get over their loss quickly, many of us believe what we're told.

Some pet keepers talk about their love for animals in a self-deprecating or joking way, for example, by calling themselves an "animal nut" or prefacing a statement about their pet with the words, "I know it's crazy, but. . . ." I've witnessed this phenomenon many times in my chaplaincy work, and research backs up this observation. Scholars who study pet keeping report that many pet keepers "employed jokes about their own relationship with their pets as a way to acknowledge [social] disapproval."[12] When we're grieving, such self-deprecating humor helps us mask our pain. We might smile and say we're okay even when we feel like we're dying inside. We might even deny our feelings altogether or dismiss them as an overreaction.

We're all creatures of our culture, and we're constantly absorbing messages about who and what we should love and who and what we should grieve. The fact that pet loss is disenfranchised in our society reflects our society's bias against animals—a bias that's sometimes explicit but is often felt implicitly as simply the way things are. Consequently, you might be shocked, troubled, and even ashamed by the intensity of your grief when your animal dies. You might also become acutely aware that the despair you feel doesn't square with how you think you should feel, and you may say things like, "What's wrong with me? I can't believe this hurts so bad."

A significant loss can compel us to reflect critically on our beliefs and values. We might discover that we've internalized the belief that animals are inherently less valuable than people. We might struggle to reconcile the fact that we can regard a pet as a family member and simultaneously think of them as inferior to our human family members. In turn, we might resist identifying our sadness for a lost pet as actual grief. Julie Carson, an Episcopal priest who studied veterinary chaplaincy with me, commented on this phenomenon in her work supporting the pet keepers in her congregation. "It was interesting to get folks to admit that their grief for pets is actual grief, which can be just as deep as grief for a human," Julie told me. "It takes a lot of reassurance and drawing out for some folks to get them to talk about pet loss, but getting to that point can be very healing and affirming."

A young man I met in my pet loss support group experienced a great deal of internal dissonance when his dog died. A lifelong animal lover, he'd worked as a vet tech and in shelters, and he'd lost many animals over the years. But he was still shocked at how painful it was to lose this particular dog. "I was really hard on myself," he said. "I was shocked at how painful it was. I seriously could not function. I mean, I knew he was going to pass away. I'd been around lots of deaths of animals before. When I worked in the shelter, I saw twenty dogs a day die. But I still felt like, 'This is just a dog, what is wrong with you?'"

When I spoke with this young man, I encouraged him to listen to his heart. When our actual feelings don't square with expectations of how we believe we should feel, we often assume that we're the one with the problem. But I would argue that the problem that needs correcting is our culture's misplaced belief that people who grieve for animals are not worthy of the same sympathy as people who grieve for human loved ones. Your love for a dog or a cat or a horse or a turtle is no less real and no less precious because the object of your affection is an animal. And it's not strange or odd or wrong to grieve intensely for a pet who was an important part of your daily life.

## CHAPTER 7

# A Spiritual Void

I met Bob Coulson when he participated in my veterinary chaplaincy course. In his mid-sixties, Bob was an affable, even-tempered man, a dedicated student, and a consistently supportive presence in our weekly Zoom discussions. A minister in the United Methodist Church and an experienced chaplain, Bob always lit a candle on his desk for our meetings in honor of the sacredness of the stories we shared about our pets.

Bob's interest in veterinary chaplaincy was sparked by the loss of his Chihuahua, Pixie. "Pixie was always with me," Bob told me when we spoke. "She became my dog. She bonded with me for some reason, even though she was a Valentine's Day gift for my wife."

In 2006 Bob was diagnosed with non-Hodgkin lymphoma, not long after Pixie joined his family. Pixie was a huge support for him during his cancer treatment. "When you do chemotherapy, your body doesn't smell quite right," Bob said. "Pixie would always get up on the back of the sofa and sit right on the back of my neck, even though I was very sick. We spent a good many hours together as I went through the treatment, which took several months in 2006. Then in 2008, the cancer came back. I always say the first time was rough, but the second time was pure hell because I had a stem cell transplant. It was a really rough time in my life, and even after I finally cleared the cancer, it took me about two years to get my stamina back. Pixie was with me through all that."

Bob's devotion to Pixie and her devotion to him opened his eyes to the power of the human-animal bond. He had always liked animals and kept pets throughout his life, but his powerful connection with Pixie was new. So was the heartbreak he felt when Pixie was diagnosed with an aggressive form of cancer, and Bob and his wife made the tough decision to have her euthanized.

"I had to love her enough to let her go," Bob said. "I understood what sacrificial love was. The veterinarian offered all these extreme measures, these cancer treatments. But having gone through that, I was not going to put Pixie through that. It was sixteen years to the day, Valentine's Day to be exact, that Pixie left us. I had her in my arms, and Diane and I were both crying. I sang her a song, a nighttime song. It was a tough experience because, as they administered the medication, she was snarling at them. Then, finally, she did go to sleep right here on my chest."

Distraught over Pixie's death, Bob turned to his spiritual leader at his church for support. That encounter proved to be a rude awakening. "I'll never forget what he said," Bob said. "His answer to me was, 'Well, when you get off your pity pot, make sure you flush.'" And I said, "Well, okay, we're done talking. Thanks anyhow."

Although Bob was shocked by his spiritual leader's response, he told me they're still good friends. After much soul-searching, he concluded that the root of the problem lies in our education system. Like his spiritual leader, Bob had received extensive training as a minister and chaplain, but his religious education focused solely on grief over the loss of people. Until he lost Pixie, he was unaware of the soul-crushing sorrow people sometimes suffer when they lose a pet. "It really struck me that in all my religious education and training, pet loss had never come up," Bob said. "I realized that if I experienced the intensity of something like this—the intensity of what I felt when I lost

Pixie—then others have had that same intensity. I realized that many people who lose pets walk through their season of sorrow alone. That's not what spiritual care is about."

What Bob experienced is a troubling example of what I call *religious disenfranchisement*. Compared to the disenfranchised grief discussed in the last chapter, religious disenfranchisement receives much less attention in the academic world. There is little, if any, research into this phenomenon, though I believe it's very real and probably more common than we realize. In this chapter, we'll explore the phenomenon of religious disenfranchisement in the pet-keeping community. I'll focus primarily on Christianity because of the simple fact that most people in the West, currently about two-thirds of US adults, identify as Christian.[1] This is not to say that pet keepers who follow other faith traditions don't suffer religious disenfranchisement, because I expect that many do. Regardless of a person's religious beliefs and practices, however, the toll of spiritual disenfranchisement for pet loss is the same—a loss of connection with a faith community and, potentially, a loss of hope as well.

## Plumbing the Depths of the Spiritual Void

Religious scholar Barbara Ambros describes the scarcity of formal religious support for pet keepers in the West as a "spiritual void."[2] An expert in animals and religion, Ambros has written extensively about modern death rites for animals. In a chapter in *The Routledge History of Death Since 1800*, she writes that "despite the development of a robust pet funeral industry, connections with institutionalized religion—so prevalent in the case of human death—remain relatively rare, or rather they are difficult to trace because they often occur in an ad hoc manner as individual religious professionals may choose to accommodate pet owners who request memorial rituals for their deceased companion animals. From mainstream doctrinal perspectives, pet funerals—let alone pet cemeteries on the grounds of religious institutions or within confessional human cemeteries—tend to present theological challenges."[3]

As Ambros observes, empirical research on pet keepers' experiences in their places of worship, and specifically on the quality of the grief support offered by their religious leaders and fellow congregants, is hard to find. What research there is indicates that such support is scarce or inconsistent. A study comparing memorial services and rituals for companion animals in Japan, Poland, and the US found that "official religious support for the grieving animal guardians seems to be scarce even in multi-faith countries such as Australia . . . or the United States of America."[4] As of this writing in 2025, the Episcopal Church is the only Christian denomination that offers a formal liturgy for pet loss.[5] While the websites of most Christian denominations and other religious institutions acknowledge that pets are important to us, they offer little in the way of guidance or support when a pet is lost.

Anecdotally, I came across an example of religious disenfranchisement in the book *Good Grief: Finding Peace After Pet Loss* by Sid Korpi.[6] While researching her book, Korpi submitted requests to a dozen religious leaders in her Minnesota community, asking for their perspectives on animals and the afterlife, among other issues. She received only three responses: from a Christian minister in a Wesleyan Church (a Methodist denomination), a Jewish rabbi, and an Eckankar leader (Eckankar is a New Age religion founded in Minnesota in 1965). The Christian minister who responded to Korpi's request took a position that appears to be typical of mainstream Christian leaders:

> Animals matter to God and to us, but the Bible does not give us the same assurance that we will be reunited with them as we expect to be with our loved ones. I certainly do not minimize the pain of losing a beloved pet, but I have no Scriptural grounds for promising someone that they will someday be with them again, though that could happen. . . . As with anything God gives, we must beware of taking pets beyond

what God intends; for example, perhaps in elevating them to the same importance and giving them the same devotion as we do to humans.[7]

When asked if he would perform a memorial service for a pet, this pastor said he would be willing to do so only in private with the person or family. He did not offer reasons for declining to publicly acknowledge the loss of a pet. Perhaps he was worried that he would offend other members of his congregation or that by honoring a pet he would diminish the stature of deceased people. It's also possible that memorializing an animal would break with the official policy of his religious institution. The rabbi who responded to Korpi's request offered a similar response, writing that "I have not and I probably would not [perform a service for a pet's passing]."[8]

Some religious leaders are openly critical of pet keeping. A prominent example is the late Pope Francis. Although animal lovers applauded Francis in 2006 when he wrote that "clearly, the Bible has no place for a tyrannical anthropocentrism unconcerned for other creatures," Francis later criticized modern pet-keeping practices.[9] In a 2022 Vatican speech, Francis referred to pet keeping as a "form of selfishness" because couples were keeping pets rather than having children.[10] When the audience tittered at this comment, Francis paused. "Yes, it's funny, I understand, but it is the reality," he said. "And this denial of fatherhood or motherhood diminishes us. It takes away our humanity." To be labeled as selfish and described as "funny" because you keep pets but have chosen not to have children is an oversimplification of a complex decision. For some pet-keeping Catholics, I can only imagine that these comments must have been troubling, if not offensive.

In my experience, the support people receive in their religious communities when they lose a pet is, at best, unpredictable. Some are privately troubled by their religious leader's dismissive attitude but continue to participate in their religious communities. Others leave their place of worship when told that their pet does not have a soul and will not go to heaven. On the other hand, a few people have told me they felt very supported in their place of worship. A Jewish woman said she was hesitant to ask for a prayer for her deceased cat in her synagogue but was surprised to find that her fellow congregants were sympathetic once she spoke up. Another acquaintance said that her Methodist minister conducted a brief remembrance ceremony for her dog during regular church services. Apparently, her minister was a dog lover, which appeared to make all the difference.

I'm always encouraged when I meet pet keepers who've had a positive experience in their place of worship. These stories give me hope that the day will arrive when we can count on the support of our religious leaders and fellow congregants when a beloved pet is lost. As it is, however, most religious institutions appear to be catching up with the public's changing views about animals. Many people seem to make up their own minds about what they hold sacred in this world, and for thousands, if not millions, animals are sacred beings worthy of our care and compassion.

## Sacred Creatures

Research on people's spiritual beliefs about animals is limited. The studies that have been done indicate that most people consider animals' lives sacred, and about half also believe that animals have an afterlife. Notably, these attitudes were common among people who participated in a mainstream religion as well as those who didn't.

A study by social scientists at North Carolina State University (NCSU) offers some interesting insights into the spiritual beliefs of a random sample of Americans.[11] The survey posed a series of questions related to religious beliefs, including whether people and animals have an afterlife; whether animals have souls and their degree of certainty about human and animal afterlife; and the extent to which a belief in the afterlife extended to all animals, including insects. The results of this study, along with an ABC News poll on this topic, are summarized below.[12]

*Almost half of survey participants believed animals definitely or probably have souls.* In contrast, only 32 percent said animals definitely or probably did not have souls. The remaining 20 percent were undecided.

*Almost half of survey participants believed animals have an afterlife.* This result is in keeping with the ABC News poll, which found participants were almost evenly split when asked whether pets enjoy an afterlife: 43 percent said yes, 40 percent said no, and 17 percent had no opinion.[13] Another interesting finding is that participants who believed in an afterlife for animals extended this belief to all species, including fish, snakes, spiders, worms, and insects.

*People who believed in an afterlife for humans were very likely to believe in an afterlife for animals.* Nearly 60 percent of participants in the NCSU study believed in an afterlife. Of these, 75 percent believed in animal afterlife. The study also found that people are more certain that humans will enjoy an afterlife and less certain that animals will enjoy the same fate.

*Women were more likely to believe in an afterlife for animals than men.* Slightly more than half of the women surveyed believed that animals have an afterlife compared to 36 percent of men.

*People who practiced Eastern religions, such as Buddhism, firmly believed in animal afterlife.* Almost 80 percent of Buddhists who participated in the NCSU study believed in an animal afterlife compared to 61 percent of mainstream Protestants and Catholics and 23 percent of individuals who indicated "none" for their religion.

*People who kept pets were somewhat more likely to believe that animals enjoy an afterlife than people who didn't keep pets.* The NCSU study found that 45 percent of pet keepers thought animals have an afterlife, compared to 38 percent of non-pet keepers. The ABC News poll reported similar results, with 47 percent of pet keepers believing in pet afterlife, compared with 38 percent among people who didn't keep pets.[14]

Like the NCSU research, a study of pet loss in Australia found that pet keepers have diverse views about animals and the afterlife.[15] Some participants totally rejected the idea ("Do I think he is chasing balls in doggy heaven? That is ridiculous. Of course not.") to total agreement ("We both believed that Simon went to a beautiful cat heaven"). Some participants stated that a belief in the afterlife was comforting but hesitated to say they believed it, while others drew a sharp boundary between people and animals ("You accept that humans live on. Pets and animals come into a different category, and I view them as having no soul that lives on"). In contrast, other study participants explicitly stated they believed both people and animals have an afterlife. Several participants said they did not consider their personal beliefs on this question to have anything to do with their religion ("My religion has no bearing on this as I believe when an animal or a human dies, our soul continues to live").

In my experience, many Christians believe that animals have souls, and many also hope to be reunited with their animals in the afterlife. As a veterinary chaplain, I've learned that questions about animals' souls and the afterlife are common among people whose faith is important to them. In fact, one of the main questions people ask me when they learn about my work is whether I believe animals go to heaven. There's no easy answer to this query because, as we'll see, the Bible doesn't explicitly say that animals ascend to heaven, although it also doesn't say that they don't.

## Do Animals Go to Heaven?

One of my first calls as the chaplain at NCSU's veterinary teaching hospital came from a veterinarian in Virginia who had recently euthanized a client's cat. The cat's human, a woman named Cynthia, was heartbroken and kept calling the veterinarian for help. The issue eventually made its way through the veterinary community until it arrived at NCSU, and my pager went off.

When I called Cynthia, I learned that her cat Leo had recently died, and that it had been almost precisely a year after her husband William had passed away from a massive heart attack. William had doted on the cat, so I knew it was likely that Cynthia's grief was complicated by the grief she still felt for her late husband. After a lengthy conversation about Leo and William, we finally arrived at the question Cynthia really wanted to ask. I remember that I had to hold the phone closer to my ear to make sure I'd heard her correctly.

In a whisper, Cynthia said, "Do you think Leo and my husband are together in heaven?"

"What do you think?" I whispered back, following her lead.

"I think they are," she replied.

"I think you're right," I affirmed.

Cynthia was quiet for a moment and then told me that knowing Bob and Leo were together in heaven was a great comfort. She thanked me for the call, and we concluded our discussion. The fact that Cynthia whispered that single question about her cat and her husband in heaven, as if she were ashamed or afraid to ask, was a clue that she was probably struggling to reconcile her faith's teachings with what her heart was telling her. All she needed was an affirmation from someone she perceived as a religious authority, a chaplain, to put her heart at ease.

Many Christian pet keepers hope to be reunited with their pets in the afterlife yet remain uncertain about their pets' fate. Many are hungry for answers. I recently searched for the best-selling self-help books on pet loss on Amazon. Six of the top ten titles examined the animal afterlife and the ability of people to connect with their deceased pets through an invisible veil separating the earthly and spiritual realms. The popularity of these books attests to the fact that most Christian denominations offer little certainty about this important question. At present, the Mormon Church appears to be the only Christian denomination that states unequivocally that animals go to heaven. In a conference address delivered in 1928, church president Joseph Fielding Smith said that "the animals, the fishes of the sea, the fowls of the air, as well as man, are to be recreated, or renewed, through the resurrection, for they too are living souls."[16]

The lack of clarity in the Christian faith on this matter has a lot to do with the Bible itself. Like many sacred texts, the Bible is full of stories, myths, and metaphors, and it's possible to find passages that appear to support the idea that animals do, in fact, have a place in heaven. Yet a review of Christian websites and published doctrine shows that the debate about animals and the afterlife is inconsistent and continually changing. In general, the more fundamentalist or evangelical Christian denominations are against the idea that animals ascend to heaven after they die. Mainline Protestant denominations emphasize the importance of treating animals with compassion but draw the line when it comes to belief in animal souls or the presence of animals in heaven. An article about animals and the afterlife on the UMC website alludes to St. Aquinas's position that animals lack rational souls: "We, as United Methodists, say that we don't believe that animals have souls. What we're really saying is animals do not or are not in need of God's redemption and forgiveness, like humans are. Instead, what we affirm when we bless animals in the church is that they are part of God's good creation."[17] In my experience, most Christian ministers fail to distinguish between rational and sentient souls; they simply say that animals don't have souls, period.

It's important to note, however, that the UMC does promote the idea of a "new earth," or the belief that God will one day recreate the entire earth as an eternal sanctuary for all life, much like the original Garden of Eden. John Wesley, the founder of the Methodist Church, espoused this view in a sermon titled "New Creation."[18] He also purportedly believed that he would one day see his beloved horse when the new earth is created. Similarly, Billy Graham, a prominent evangelical leader and dog lover, famously asserted that if his happiness in heaven depended on his dog's presence, then God would make sure his dog was there. This position doesn't abandon the dominant Christian belief that God created animals to serve human needs. As stated on the Billy Graham ministry website, "We believe that animals were intended for man's enjoyment and use. The Bible itself does not indicate that there is life after death for animals. It may be that God's purpose for animals is fulfilled on this earth. However, if animals would make us happier in heaven, surely there will be a place for them there."[19]

As previously noted, the Catholic Church has long maintained the position that animals have sentient souls that don't ascend to heaven after death; rather, the animal's soul ceases to exist. As discussed in chapter 4, this position originated with St. Augustine and St. Aquinas in medieval Europe. It was affirmed in the late nineteenth century when Pope Pius IX officially declared that animals are soulless (and even lacking in consciousness) and are thus unable to enter heaven. According to psychologist Stanley Coren, Pope Pius IX "led a heated campaign to try to prevent the founding of the Italian Society for the Prevention of Cruelty to Animals on the grounds that animals have no souls. Pius quoted Thomas Aquinas to prove his case, since Aquinas often noted that animals are not beings, but just 'things.'"[20]

Since then, popes have waffled on the issue. In the 1970s, Pope Paul VI was said to have once told a distraught boy whose dog had died that "one day, we will see our animals again in the eternity of Christ. Paradise is open to all of God's creatures."[21] But in 2008, Pope Benedict XVI stated that God only gives access to heaven to people, asserting that when an animal dies, it just means the end of its existence on earth.[22] Then in 2016, Pope Francis veered sharply toward a more open position on this topic when he issued his Laudato Si' encyclical letter, wrote that "eternal life will be a shared experience of awe, in which each creature, resplendently transfigured, will take its rightful place and have something to give those poor men and women who will have been liberated once and for all."[23] Encyclicals are considered official church doctrine, yet the debate about animals' souls and the afterlife continued in Catholic communities after the release of Laudato Si'. Some Catholic commentators embraced Pope Francis's animal-friendly position while others struck a middle ground of tentative but critical acceptance. Yet many detractors also forcefully challenged the encyclical's stance on animals and creation.

The Catholic Church's waffling on the question of animal souls and the afterlife is a good example of the lack of clarity evident in the Christian faith as a whole and the considerable confusion many Christian pet keepers experience. Depending on where you worship and who you talk to, you might be told that, yes, God loves all creation, and, because God's creatures matter to God, they matter to us as well, but no, sorry, animals don't go to heaven because they lack rational souls, although on the other hand, maybe they do go to heaven but only because people need them to be happy. It's enough to make your head spin.

I don't mean to make light of this troubling situation. If my attitude seems flippant, I suppose it reflects the disillusionment I've personally experienced with today's Christian institutions and the apparent lack of concern for animals and the natural world. The point is that religiously active pet keepers who've fallen into the West's spiritual void are deprived of the hope that they will one day be reunited with their beloved pets in the afterlife. They're also deprived of one of the most important social connections they possess—a community of people who share and celebrate a common conception of the universe and the divine.

## The Toll of Religious Disenfranchisement

Research shows that people who believe they will one day be reunited with their loved ones in the afterlife tend to find acceptance and peace sooner and more easily than people who don't have such beliefs. In a review of research about the benefits of religious practice for mental health, researcher and author Dr. Deborah Cornah outlines the benefits of religious practices when we're coping with the loss of a loved one.[24] This includes a "collaborative approach to religious coping" wherein individuals call on God to help them with their loss. Cornah also notes that our faith traditions help us reframe uncontrollable events as part of God's universal order, offering a meaningful interpretation for death as the continuation of life in a more peaceful realm. Sacred texts are replete with positive language that offers solace to survivors, encouraging them to embrace teachings about hope, contentment, love, and forgiveness. Finally, Cornah asserts that spiritual music, art, and the splendid architecture of many places of worship often inspire a sense of awe and a connection with the divine, which can be comforting when a loved one is lost.

Neurological studies have shown that religious or spiritual practice is highly beneficial to people, both cognitively and physiologically. In *How God Changes Your Brain: Breakthrough Findings from a Leading Neuroscientist*, Dr. Andrew Newberg has verified that people who regularly pray or practice meditation (whether spiritual or secular) have decreased activity in the part of the brain that constructs our sense of an independent self, helping us feel less isolated and more connected with one another and the world around us. Newberg's research also affirms that "activity involving meditation and intensive prayer permanently strengthens neural functioning in specific parts of the brain that are involved with lowering anxiety and depression, enhancing social awareness and empathy, and improving cognitive and intellectual functioning."[25]

Religious or spiritual beliefs and practices also offer many practical benefits to grieving people. Many pet keepers seek guidance from religious texts when making health-care decisions for their animals, particularly when they're considering euthanasia. One study found that, for nearly half of US pet keepers, their religious or spiritual beliefs either moderately or strongly influenced the decisions they made at the end of their animal's life.[26] In all measures—from the decision to euthanize to how to handle their pet's remains to the way they choose to memorialize their pet—the number of people who said their religious or spiritual beliefs either moderately or strongly influenced their preferences exceeded the number who said their beliefs had no impact on these decisions. Another US study found that, of all the options available for memorializing pets, such as displaying a photo of a pet or keeping some of a pet's hair or fur, the most comforting was the feeling that they would be reunited with their animal in the afterlife.[27]

The point is that our faith traditions have traditionally played a critical role in helping us navigate the loss of a loved one. When our religious institutions do not officially support the prospect of an afterlife for animals, the journey of grief and healing can potentially be much more difficult for people who long to meet their pets in heaven. Of course, religious disenfranchisement for pet loss is nothing new, so most people who are active in a faith community are conditioned not to expect support from their religious leaders or fellow congregants. My concern is for those people who need spiritual support when they lose a pet but who remain silent and grieve alone or are rebuffed or even ridiculed when they reach out for help.

## An Untold Story

The disconnect between the West's mainstream religious institutions and animals is not confined to those species commonly kept as pets. An increasing number of people grieve not only for the loss of their animal companions but for the suffering of those animals we use for food and experimentation, the extinction of wild animals, and the despoiling of the earth. Hence, the separation of church and pet described here is, in fact, the separation of church and animal and the separation of church and nature.

As discussed in chapter 4, this separation can be traced to Aristotelian metaphysics, or the Great Chain of Being, which was eventually incorporated into Christian doctrine by St. Thomas Aquinas in the thirteenth century. The editors of *Animals and Religion*, a scholarly work published in 2024, allude to this historical connection in this passage:

> Western thought has often imagined religion as part of a vertical movement above the ordinary, biological, deterministic, and mundane—in a word, the animal—aspects of existence. The dominant Western heritage imagined a great chain of being stretching from the inanimate to the animal, and then beyond these, to the higher planes of humanity and, ultimately, divinity; anything that might be called religious was located on these higher planes. Historically, the vast majority of Christian theologians and, later, most scientifically-minded scholars of religion have argued, or just assumed, that religion begins where animality ends.[28]

Religious disenfranchisement among pet keepers can be attributed in part to institutional inertia. Many Christian denominations appear to be bound by traditional, anthropocentric interpretations of biblical teachings, and they've been slow to respond to substantive changes in their congregants' daily lives and pressing concerns. They've also neglected meaningful and regular engagement in critical discussions about sacred teachings, animals, and the natural world.

My own religious experiences speak to this phenomenon. I no longer attend church, but I was raised Catholic and received infant baptism and confirmation, heard priests read scripture in Latin, and received religious instruction, or catechism, as a child. As an adult, I spent fifteen years at a liberal Baptist church, where I received adult baptism and spent a great deal of time studying the Bible. I also spent three years living with my spiritual mentor as part of an informal community of former seminarians and others like me exploring our spiritual paths. For nearly twenty years, I attended an annual interfaith conference, where I joined leaders from Jewish, Christian, Muslim, and other faiths as they discussed sacred texts and sought common ground. This has been the foundation of my religious education, and in sixty years, I cannot recall a single sermon dedicated solely to sacred teachings about animals and the earth.

This fact troubles me deeply, though I admit I did not always feel this way. For most of my life, I never really gave much thought to the absence of animals and the earth in the religious dialogue I was exposed to. Most mainstream books on Christianity have little to do with animals or the natural world. It's as if someone came along with a big red pen and deleted every mention of animals and nature from our collective spiritual story. Once I became aware of this void in the Christian worldview, I noticed it everywhere.

Even progressive Christian writers tend to perpetuate the idea that God is solely concerned with human affairs. A good example is Christian scholar Cynthia Bourgeault, who is regarded as a modern-day mystic. Historically, Christian mystics were among the most devoted lovers of animals and nature in the Christian world. I cannot say the same of Bourgeault. In her book *The Wisdom Jesus*, Bourgeault argues for a paradigm shift in our understanding of Jesus as a wisdom teacher and offers valuable insights into the power of contemplative prayer to help us connect with the divine.[29] I enjoyed the book but was disappointed to find echoes of a familiar anti-animal bias. Bourgeault asserts, for example, that we must seek to transform "our animal instincts and egocentricity into love and compassion."[30] This kind of language depicts animal instincts as somehow the opposite of, or at least incompatible with, love and compassion. She also describes Aristotle's Great Chain of Being as a "classic wisdom schematic" and, in discussing her approach to contemplative prayer and meditation, emphasizes the image of an evolutionary ladder in which people are ascendant.[31]

I realize it was not Bourgeault's purpose to explicate animal theology in *The Wisdom Jesus*. Yet I believe the casual way in which she treats the topic perpetuates some common tropes, such as the belief that animals can never enjoy a heightened state of consciousness that enables them to connect directly with God as people do and that we must actively suppress our own animal-ness and control our unruly emotions if we're to connect with the divine.

Broadly speaking, most Christian denominations in the contemporary West focus on New Testament teachings, which concern the life of Jesus Christ and offer guidance for achieving salvation. Much less attention is given to the Old Testament, where most teachings specific to the treatment of animals and God's creation are found. I remember visiting my older brother Rick, who as an adult became a devout Southern Baptist. When we talked about our religious beliefs, he liked to flip through his Bible, and one day I noticed that the New Testament portion of his Bible was dog-eared and worn from much use, while the Old Testament portion had barely been touched.

Years later, my observations about contemporary Christianity were confirmed when I read *Cold Noses at the Pearly Gates* by Gary Kurz, a long-time Baptist who was intimately familiar with the Bible.[32] Kurz described how he pored through the Bible he knew so well, looking for scripture that supported his hope that animals go to heaven. He didn't find a straightforward answer but was surprised to discover a wealth of beautiful teachings about animals he'd never noticed before. "I simply love the Bible, and I love learning new things from it," wrote Kurz. "I began seeing things about animals that I had never seen before. It absolutely staggered me that I had spent so much time in the Bible and had never paid attention to this subject."[33]

As Kurz astutely observed, numerous passages in the Bible speak to God's love for animals and the need for us to respect our fellow creatures. But mainstream religious institutions have largely neglected these teachings, and this omission perpetuates the belief that humans are God's sole concern and are the only life-form that warrants moral consideration. In my view, this absence is a great disservice not only to animals and the earth but also to people.

The failure of our religious institutions to respond to the needs of their animal-loving congregants is a missed opportunity *and* a missed calling. Melissa M. Kelley, assistant professor of pastoral care and counseling at the Boston College Clough School of Theology and Ministry, describes this call for care when she writes that "ministers and faith communities have a particular responsibility to ensure that no grieving persons in their midst go unrecognized and unsupported. In Matthew 5:4, we hear Jesus' all-embracing words of solace, 'Blessed are those who mourn, for they will be comforted.' Jesus did not single out certain groups of mourners as deserving comfort. He blessed all those who grieve."[34]

Pet chaplaincy is my answer to this call. My goal is to bring our animal companions more prominently into our spiritual lives. This is not to say that pets need to attend worship with us, though this is taking place on a very limited basis and only when a church or temple has facilities to accommodate congregants' pets. But I see great value in formally honoring our pets when they're sick or dying as well as providing spiritual support for each other when we lose them. Beyond this, the bigger issue in my mind is the need for religious leaders to think more inclusively in their sermons and broaden the messages they deliver about animals and the earth beyond a passing mention of lions lying down with lambs or the occasional nod to Earth Day.

## Bridging the Spiritual Void

Like so many aspects of our lives, our religious institutions are changing. Over the last fifty years, many new voices have emerged that challenge the anthropocentric worldview that has long characterized

Western religious institutions. As noted earlier, the Episcopal Church was the first mainstream Christian denomination in the US to officially adopt liturgies for commemorating the loss of a pet, including prayers for the loss of a pet along with additional prayers for companion and service animals.[35] At least forty-five Episcopal Churches have established pet memorial gardens on church grounds, and most of these emerged since 2010.[36] This is good news for Episcopal pet lovers, and it's possible that, as more pet keepers seek a spiritual response to the loss of their animals, other places of worship may follow suit.

Some Jewish denominations are beginning to offer creative ways for their members to memorialize their pets, although the actual internment of animals on temple grounds is still forbidden. In a review of pet-oriented programs in Jewish synagogues, religious studies scholar Barbara Ambros cites a few examples, including the Reform Temple Beth Emet in Cooper City, Florida, which has a pet memorial garden where congregants can place a memorial stone in remembrance of their companion animal; the Reform Congregation Kol Ami Synagogue in West Hollywood, California, which has a pet memorial tree in its courtyard that allows congregants to dedicate leaf-shaped plaques of three sizes; and Temple Israel, a Conservative congregation in Norfolk, Virginia, which features a Pet Remembrance Board that references the popular "Rainbow Bridge" poem.[37]

Another encouraging development is the emergence of pet ministries in places of worship. A few graduates of my veterinary chaplaincy course have successfully launched animal ministries in their churches. They've organized food and fundraising drives for local animal shelters and rescue groups; funded programs that help people of limited means afford veterinary care; hosted humane education programs for children; and created pet loss support groups, among other activities.

Blessing of the animals events are also increasing in number and popularity, particularly in Reform Jewish communities in the US and in Christian places of worship worldwide. At such events, religious leaders bless the animals in attendance and deliver sermons that celebrate and honor all of God's creation. Today, most of the animals who participate in such blessings are pets, but at the Cathedral of Saint John the Divine in New York City, which holds one of the world's biggest and most popular blessing events each October, the procession of animals has included "eagles, camels, llamas, hedgehogs, bees, and more (almost all from local sanctuaries or rescue groups)."[38]

According to Laura Hobgood, professor of environmental studies and religion at Southwestern University, animal blessings are occurring in "many countries with substantial Christian populations, including Italy, Kenya, the Philippines, Mexico, Peru, and more. Animal blessings are indeed becoming a more global phenomenon in the Christian tradition."[39] These events offer important ways for churches and temples to engage with the local community and attract new congregants:

> The blessings of pets attract people who are not necessarily members of the congregation offering the event. Frequently, pet rescue groups or animal activist organizations participate in the blessing itself and/or in a larger event connected with it. Congregations might advertise fairly widely, inviting the larger community to join them. Also, as environmental concerns become linked more closely to religious concerns in many Jewish and Christian communities, the blessing of pets indicates a way to connect with creation overall. On a different note, some evangelical churches frame the blessings as a way to attract young people to the church.[40]

I participated for a few years as a chaplain at the blessing of the animals held at the Duke University Chapel in Durham, North Carolina. The blessing was held in a large grassy courtyard in front of the Gothic chapel's stone entrance. Many people brought their lawn chairs and, of course, their dogs. Cats were rare, since most don't do well in crowded public events, but birds, snakes, and even exotic animals like iguanas were sometimes present. The animals seemed to sense the significance of the occasion and were remarkably well behaved. People and animals alike were enchanted by the ethereal voices from local children's choirs, whose performances were interspersed with scriptural readings and reflections from church leadership.

The developments described here signal a slow but steady shift in the spiritual void that has long characterized the relationship between the West's mainstream faith traditions and animals. There's a great need for the kind of spiritual support that churches, temples, and other places of worship are uniquely positioned to provide. It's also clear that many religiously active pet keepers—as well as those who don't regularly participate in organized religion—regard their animals as sacred beings and wish to honor them in familiar and comforting ways when they're lost. I applaud the changes some of the West's mainstream religious institutions are making to support their animal-loving congregants, and I hope that many more will follow.

• • •

It's been more than two thousand years since Aristotle placed humans at the top of a metaphysical ladder and positioned animals and all other life-forms further down the ladder. To this day, however, these age-old conceptions about animals continue to guide our interactions with them, particularly on an institutional level. When the early Christian church declared that we owed no moral obligation to other life-forms and René Descartes stated that animals were nothing more than complex machines, our natural inclination to dominate our fellow creatures was given free rein. Animals have paid a heavy price for this reality, and people have suffered as well, particularly those who feel a kinship with animals and are concerned for their well-being.

The cost of our long-standing anthropocentric mindset—both to ourselves and animals—is impossible to quantify. Yet it is also becoming impossible to turn a blind eye to the unhappy consequences of our society's habitual anti-animal bias. As noted in the introduction, I believe we're in the midst of a vast paradigm shift in our relationship with animals and the natural world. As we'll see in the coming chapters, this shift is taking place in how we think about ourselves and other life-forms in the cosmos, what we consider sacred and worthy of moral consideration, how we conceive of the soul, and our understanding of the spiritual and physical realms. This shift is also occurring in the scientific world as researchers gain new insights into the inner lives of nonhuman animals. Although these shifts are slow and even painful, they signal that a new era may be unfolding in the ongoing evolution of the human-animal bond.

CHAPTER 5–7

# Discussion Questions

1. Of the three topics discussed in chapter 5—pets as ersatz people, animals as property, and the pet industry—select one that is particularly concerning to you and describe why you selected it. If you've had a personal experience with any of these situations, tell a story that explains what happened and how you felt about it.

2. In chapter 6, we learned that people who love and care for animals are socially disenfranchised in Western society. Describe an interaction you've had with a person who views animals differently from you and how you felt about that interaction.

3. Tell a brief story about an interaction with someone when you minimized, hid, or joked about your feelings for animals. Next, tell a brief story about when you were honest about your feelings for animals with another person. Compare and contrast these two experiences.

4. Chapter 7 explored the religious disenfranchisement of pet keepers. Have you or someone you know been disenfranchised in a place of worship when a pet was lost? Describe what happened and how you feel about this experience. Next, describe an experience in a place of worship that felt supportive of your feelings about animals or the grief you experienced for the loss of a pet. If you don't participate in organized religion, then share your thoughts and feelings on Bob Coulson's story about his dog Pixie presented at the beginning of chapter 7.

5. If you're currently active in a religious community or were active in the past, how would you describe the perspective about animals

and the natural world promoted in your place of worship? If you've never participated in organized religion, do you believe that religious institutions should be more active in this regard? Why or why not?

# A Changing Cultural Landscape

## CHAPTER 8

# The Evolving Spiritual Narrative About Animals

In 1789 Jeremy Bentham, an English philosopher and social reformer, offered a succinct statement that highlights the growing concern for animal welfare in Western society. "The question," Bentham wrote, "is not can [animals] reason, nor can they talk, but can they suffer?"[1] At that time, the Industrial Revolution was picking up steam in Europe and the US, and animals were used mercilessly for their labor. Their suffering was impossible for ordinary people to ignore, especially in urban areas where horses and oxen were often worked to death.

Bentham's ethical declaration was a rallying cry for citizens who were horrified by the cruel treatment of animals, and a social movement began to take shape. England's Royal Society for the Prevention of Cruelty to Animals (RSPCA), the world's first animal welfare charity, was founded in a London coffee shop in 1824 by a group of Christian clergy and social reformers. Over the next forty years, sister organizations sprang up in Scotland, Ireland, America, and New Zealand. In response to lobbying from Christian anti-vivisectionists, Britain passed the Cruelty to Animals Act in 1876, which was the first piece of national legislation to regulate animal experimentation. The heartfelt concern for the plight of animals was also popularized by books such as *Black Beauty*.[2] Written by English author Anna Sewell in 1877, the novel tells the story of a horse's life from the horse's perspective, forthrightly promoting the idea that animals are self-aware and intelligent. *Black Beauty* became an immediate bestseller. With more than fifty million copies sold to date, it's one of the best-selling books of all time.

Today, a vast cultural movement focused on protecting animals and improving their lives is once again taking shape. As noted by ecowriter Richard Louv, "In kind, loving, conflicted ways, people are reaching out to animals, our fellow travelers. Around the world, good-hearted people are becoming the New Noahs, creating new habitats for wild animals or operating rescue centers for abused dogs and birds with broken wings. As animals save us, we discover new ways to save animals."[3]

This movement is vast and diverse. Animal ethicists have picked up Jeremy Bentham's torch of justice and are developing ethical frameworks that constrain the excesses of an unruly, profit-driven economic system that continues to treat most animals solely as commodities. Christian theologians question the dominionist mandate interpretation of the Bible and offer a more equitable vision of animals within the kingdom of God. Artists and writers touch people's hearts with images and words that remind us of our connection with animals and our moral obligation to protect them. Animal rights and welfare advocates are working to prevent the suffering of billions of animals in factory farms and animal testing labs and mitigate the widespread environmental destruction fueled by factory farming. Animal rights attorneys challenge a legal system that categorizes animals as property with limited rights and protections. Animal rescue workers educate the pet-keeping public about the realities of pet keeping and continue their efforts to find forever homes for millions of unhomed animals. Veterinarians and animal hospice teams provide in-home care and euthanasia services that ensure our pets are comfortable at the end of their lives. Holistic healers, from Reiki practitioners to acupuncturists, seek less invasive approaches to animal health care. Ethologists and biologists spend years in remote locations studying wild animals in their natural habitats to better understand their behavior and their inner lives. Conservationists and environmentalists create and maintain animal sanctuaries to reduce the destruction of wild habitats and stem the extinction of wild species worldwide. And, finally, ordinary people from all walks of life and diverse spiritual traditions cry out against the commodification and suffering of animals in today's profit-driven, industrialized economies. This includes Indigenous peoples in the US and Australia as well as modern-day followers of Europe's ancient pagan societies.

More than two centuries have passed since Bentham set forth his ethical challenge to the Western world. Since then, limited progress has been made to protect animal interests in our legal system and raise public awareness about the plight of animals of all kinds. Animals, including those commonly kept as pets, are arguably better off than they were in Bentham's day. Yet animal advocates are unsatisfied with the status quo, even if they don't agree entirely on what they hope to accomplish. Some are concerned with animal welfare and want to protect animals from undue suffering and early death. Others are concerned with animal rights and envision a transformed world in which animals carry out their lives as nature intended, free from human interference and constraint.

Despite their differences, people who love animals and strive to protect their interests share some common goals: to understand animals better, encourage people to respect animals, and find ways to live on this earth with greater balance and in mutually beneficial ways with our fellow creatures. Collectively, the voices of these friends of the animals are saying—and often shouting—enough is enough! It's time to wake up and realize that we're not the only creatures on this planet. We're all connected, and the survival of the human species depends on the survival of other species and care for the complex bio-systems on which we all depend.

In chapter 4, we explored some of the core ideas that have guided the dominant narrative about animals in Western society. We'll return to those ideas now and ask a simple question: What's new? What has changed and what hasn't since our forebears promoted the beliefs on which modern Western culture was built? How do we define *soul* today, and how does this differ from the perspective offered by early Christian theologians? What changes, if any, have taken place in our dualistic perspective of the cosmos, and what are the long-term consequences of this mindset? And how do modern-day Christians think about the relationship between humans and animals and their ethical obligation to animals? As we'll see, some of these ideas have changed considerably while others have not. Yet it's undeniable that countless people are questioning the anthropocentric worldview that has long characterized Western society, and our future is likely to look much different than our past.

## Redefining the Soul

One of the core ideas discussed in chapter 4 that doesn't appear to sit well with modern sensibilities is Aristotle's notion of rational and sentient souls. Today, most people appear have a much broader perspective about who has a soul and who does not. As noted earlier, the majority of Americans believe that all living beings have a soul, including insects.[4] Moreover, the word *soul* is defined in such diverse ways today that, outside of some conservative religious circles, distinguishing between rational and sentient souls seems archaic. Most people I've met in my work as a spiritual caregiver equate the concept of the soul with a living being's unique character or essential nature.

This perspective appears to have very little to do with rationality or religious doctrine. Jon Katz's book, *Soul of a Dog: Reflections on the Spirits of the Animals of Bedlam Farm*, offers a good example of this broader perspective about the concept of the soul.[5] According to Katz, his border collie, Rose, lives to work. She has little interest in affection, either with Katz, other people, or the other farm animals. For Rose, her work *is* her soul, which Katz equates with her guiding purpose in life. "Rose is about devotion to work, about service," Katz writes.[6] Katz's dog Lenore, on the other hand, is a loving black lab whose purpose in life appears to be befriending every creature she encounters, from people to insects to irascible sheep. In thinking about the souls of these very different dogs, Katz concludes that "each dog responds to what's innate in them, and also to what I ask of them. Rose works for me and Lenore loves me. That's where our souls converge."[7]

It's also worth noting that the very narrow definitions of *soul* embraced by the early Christian church don't stand up to scrutiny. You might recall that St. Thomas Aquinas asserted that our possession of a rational soul hinges on our unique ability to judge right from wrong, reflect on our behavior, and rationally account for our actions based on God's teachings. Animals were believed to lack the ability for rational thought or moral behavior. But is this actually the case? Are animals merely dumb beasts who respond in simplistic, instinctive ways to external stimuli? Or are they capable of making rational or moral choices?

In *Wild Justice: The Moral Lives of Animals*, cognitive ethologist Marc Bekoff and ethicist Jessica Pierce make a compelling case that animals who live in complex social groups have moral codes of right and wrong and good and bad behavior.[8] This includes wolves, dolphins, orcas, elephants, rats, ravens, and primates. The authors offer many examples that suggest animals have moral intelligence, describing "a rat in a cage [who] refuses to push a lever for food when it sees that another rat receives an electric shock as a result. A male Diana monkey who has learned to insert a token into a slot to obtain food helps a female who can't get the hang of the trick, inserting the token for her and allowing her to eat the food reward. . . . In a group of chimpanzees at the Arnhem Zoo in the Netherlands, individuals punish other chimpanzees who are late for dinner because no one eats until everyone is present."[9]

Closer to home, anyone who has caught their dog sneaking a treat can tell you that animals can be clever and deceptive. They also exhibit what appears to be shame when they know they've broken the rules of the pack. A feline treat thief, of course, will stare you down, nonchalantly yawning and flicking their tails as if to say, "Who me?" Clearly, more is going on in an animal's mind than our forebears believed. Like people, many animals do, in fact, demonstrate a strong sense of right and wrong and create codes of conduct that are essential for the cohesiveness of their social groups. Moreover, animals of all species regularly engage in empathetic and altruistic behavior, just as people do, both within and across species.

Other people think of the soul expansively, as something that connects us with all living beings. It's like a collective soul, as if we all reside within the divine all the time. Reverend Gary Kowalski, a Unitarian Universalist minister who has written many books about theology, nature, and animals, offers some insightful reflections on the *soul* as the cosmos's connective tissue. He writes that, "many people think of soul as the element of personality that survives bodily death, but for me it refers to something much more down-to-earth. Soul is the marrow of our existence as sentient, sensitive beings. It's soul that's revealed in great works of art, and soul that's lifted up in awe when we stand in silence under a night sky burning with billions of stars. . . . Soul is what makes each of our lives a microcosm—not merely a meaningless fragment of the universe, but at some level a reflection of the whole."[10]

Clearly, conceptions of the soul today are far less restrictive than the narrow definitions offered by the early Roman Catholic church. We tend to take these ideas for granted and don't often reflect on them in depth. That is, we talk about our souls and our spirits without really understanding precisely what we mean by these common terms. We also don't consistently give much thought to the distinction between the realm of the spirit and the soul and their relationship with the physical world. So what's new in that arena of our lives? Do we still think of the soul and body as separate entities, or have new conceptions of the cosmos emerged in the modern era?

## Soul and Body, Spirit and Flesh

For most people in Western society, the belief that the spiritual and physical realms of existence are separate entities seems obvious. We tend to think of the soul or spirit as an invisible force that is distinct and separate from the physical substance of the body. This perspective is partly based on how we experience the world. Our thoughts and emotions seem immaterial or lacking in substance, so we naturally assume that they're somehow disconnected from our physical bodies. Of course, an increasing proportion of people in the modern age have challenged the idea that a spiritual realm exists at all. Yet most people habitually talk about the spiritual and physical realms of existence, even if they don't have strong spiritual or religious beliefs.

Cartesian dualism has dominated the West for centuries. Yet it's not a universal belief, and it never has been. Many Indigenous spiritual traditions assert that the physical world is suffused with spirits, a perspective that has gained ground in the West as more people become involved in neo-pagan practices such as Wicca. But even in mainstream religious practice, there have always been individuals who eschewed dualism. A good example is Benedict de Spinoza, a contemporary of Descartes, who rejected the traditional dualistic perspective of his Jewish teachers. In his magnum opus, *Ethics*, published in 1677, Spinoza defined God as a single substance containing all things and consisting of both matter and thought.[11] Known as Spinozism, this perspective claimed that nature *is* God. In keeping with this principle, Spinoza believed that humans, animals, and all of nature are "in God" and that humans should use their gift for rational thought to discover the laws of nature and live according to them.[12] These ideas were so radical and offensive to the Jewish leaders of his day that Spinoza was excommunicated in 1656 from the Jewish community in Amsterdam in which he'd grown up.

In modern times, one of the most prominent religious figures to embrace the idea that the spiritual and the physical are different aspects of the same substance is Thomas Berry. A Catholic priest, cultural historian, scholar of the world's religions, and prolific author, Berry holds a monistic rather than a dualistic conception of the cosmos, asserting that the spiritual and the physical are "two dimensions of the single reality that is the universe itself."[13] Similarly, animism, or the belief that the physical world is imbued with spirit, is common in the earth-focused spiritual traditions of Indigenous peoples, and many modern-day Wiccans and other neo-pagans also imbue the physical world with spiritual qualities.

Cartesian dualism has had a huge impact on modern society. To begin with, dualism is foundational to the belief in Christianity and other religions that the soul is eternal and lives on forever after the physical body ceases to function. Dualism is also alive and well in scientific circles. The belief that our minds are like a "ghost in the machine"—an unseen but powerful entity that animates our bodies—is foundational to the work of biomedical researchers and computer scientists who want to download the human mind like a piece of software onto a computer hard drive and eventually reboot it in another machine-like body.[14]

Although relatively few people question the basic premise of Cartesian dualism, many scholars have pointed out that this foundational idea has been profoundly harmful to ourselves, other animals, and the earth itself. Their concern lies not with the basic premise of dualism but with the way we habitually elevate and celebrate these metaphysical aspects of our existence while simultaneously denigrating the physical. This perspective has roots in Christian doctrine, which holds that the soul is divine while the physical aspects of our lives are sinful and something we should tightly control and even suppress. The reflections of Irish poet and Catholic scholar John O'Donohue in his theological treatise *Anam Cara* speak to this concern:

> The body has had such a low and negative profile in the world of spirituality because spirit has been understood more in terms of the air element than the earth element. The air is the region of the invisible; it is the region of breath and thought. When you confine spirit to this region alone, the physical becomes immediately diminished. This is a great mistake, for there is nothing in the universe as sensuous as God. . . . Nature is the direct expression of the divine imagination. It is the most intimate reflection of God's sense of beauty. Nature is the mirror of the divine imagination and the mother of all sensuality; therefore, it is unorthodox to understand spirit in terms of the invisible alone.[15]

The American writer and cultural critic Wendell Berry (who bears no relation to Thomas Berry noted above) has also been critical of the West's habitual denigration of the physical aspects of existence. "Contempt for the body," he writes, "is invariably manifested in contempt for other bodies—the bodies of slaves, laborers, women, animals, plants, the earth itself. Relationships with all other creatures become competitive and exploitive rather than collaborative and convivial. The world is seen and dealt with, not as an ecological community, but as a stock exchange."[16]

The point is that when we denigrate the physical aspects of being, we risk turning ourselves, other living beings, and the earth itself into mere objects. We may also fail to appreciate our essential physical connection with the world around us. As Berry writes, "Our bodies are not distinct from the bodies of other people, on which they depend in a complexity of ways from biological to spiritual. They are not distinct from the bodies of plants and animals, with which we are involved in the cycles of feeding and in the intricate companionships of ecological systems and of the spirit. They are not distinct from the earth, the sun and moon, and the other heavenly bodies."[17]

## Good Stewards

Nearly seventeen hundred years ago, the Christian mystic St. Basil the Great wrote a famous prayer that anticipates some of the theological themes discussed here. In his prayer, St. Basil calls on God to:

> Enlarge within us the sense of
> fellowship with all living things,
> our brothers the animals to whom you
> gave the earth as their home in
> common with us.
>
> We remember with shame that in the past
> we have exercised the high dominion
> of humans with ruthless cruelty
> so that the voice of the earth
> which should have gone up to you
> in song, has been a groan of travail.
>
> May we realize that they live not for
> us alone but for themselves and for
> you, and that they love the
> sweetness of life.[18]

Today, most Christians share St. Basil's concern for animals and the natural world, asserting that we have a moral responsibility to respect and care for animals and the earth—a belief described as responsible stewardship. When interpreting the word *dominion* in the Bible's first book of Genesis, people who embrace the principle of stewardship believe that God calls on his followers to love and care for Creation as God does. God may have given humans power over other living creatures and the earth itself, but with great power comes great responsibility. My friend Mary DeRosa, whose story about her cat Linus appears in chapter 11, told me that her love of animals and her faith are deeply intertwined. She regularly volunteers in animal rescue and draws inspiration for her work from her Christian faith. "I believe in my heart that God's original intent was for us to live in peace with the earth and the animals that God gave to us as companions," she told me. "Humans have dominion over animals, but dominion doesn't mean we have a license to abuse animals. It means being a good steward. It means to care for something. I also think God puts us here for a reason. We all have a purpose, and my purpose is to care for animals. So, my rescue work and my faith strengthen each other."

The stewardship principle has been widely adopted by Christians in the modern West. According to a study by the Pew Research Center, about three-quarters of religiously affiliated Americans say the earth is sacred, and about 80 percent completely or mostly agree with the idea that "God gave humans a duty to protect and care for the Earth, including the plants and animals."[19] The study also found that about two-thirds of American adults who identify with a religious group say "their faith's holy scriptures contain lessons about the environment, and about four-in-ten . . . say they have prayed for the environment in the past year."

The current movement in Christianity to embrace a more animal- and creation-friendly interpretation of Genesis 1 and other biblical teachings about animals and the natural world is known among theologians as *retrieval.* According to theologian Allison Covey, retrieval entails "going back to earlier texts and ideas, attempting to recover their original meaning while clearing away later misconceptions or distortions of them."[20] Over the last fifty years, an increasing number of individuals and organizations in the Christian community have challenged prevailing anthropocentric interpretations of the Bible. As noted by the editors of *Animals and Religion,* a collection of scholarly essays published in 2024, many people are embracing the idea that "a peaceful relationship between humans and other animals would be a return to the original peace described in Eden, a return to God's original plan for Creation."[21]

In the mid-1970s, Christian scholars began to take a leadership role in the animal rights and welfare movements, inheriting the torch of animal advocacy from pioneers like Jeremy Bentham. Known as animal theology, this movement was pioneered by Anglican theologian Andrew Linzey, whose seminal work, *Animal Rights: A Christian Assessment of Man's Treatment of Animals*, was published in 1976.[22] *Animal Rights* is controversial because it rejects the claim by some Christians that God is totally consumed with human purposes and that creation is simply a stage on which we work out our salvation, while animals are mere pawns to be used as we see fit.

Linzey argues that Christianity has championed negative perceptions about animals that are theologically unsupportable. He offers the example of Aristotle's Great Chain of Being, which he claims is logically flawed. He points out that the notion that we're closer to the divine than other animals because of our ability to reason assumes that animals lack the faculty of reason entirely. The Great Chain of Being also elevates the faculties of reason and logic above all other qualities, such as emotional intelligence, nonjudgmental love, and forgiveness. As a counterpoint to this perspective, Linzey asserts that God loves all creation, and humankind is called to love God's creatures as God loves them. This position is known as *theocentricity*. In contrast to anthropocentrism, theocentricity holds that "God, not humanity, is the center of all goodness. God's interests and relationship with Creation imbue all creatures with intrinsic value."[23] In supporting this claim, Linzey offers the following logic-based statement:

> If God is by definition the Creator of all things, it follows that animals are fellow creatures. Humans are not God. It follows that we do not own other creatures, and they do not belong

to us. It also necessarily follows that their worth and value to God is an entirely separate thing from their worth and value to human beings. It is difficult to imagine that God would create millions of species but care for only one of them. . . . Human interest, however vital or important, cannot be the sole basis on which we judge the morality of our relations with other creatures. The big issue always is whether God's own interest as Creator is being properly reflected in what humans do with what God has created.[24]

Linzey has written prolifically about animals and Christianity over the last fifty years. In 1999, he released a book of liturgy for animals called *Animal Rites: Liturgies of Animal Care* in which he celebrates God's love for all creation and documents the humanitarian efforts that took shape in the late 1800s and that continue to this day.[25] He writes that "creaturely fellowship [is] based on the common origin of all creatures with God; opposition to cruelty as unjust and wrong in itself; the recognition—following St. Paul—of the travail and suffering of fellow creatures; and last, but not least, the rejection of a wholly instrumentalist view of animals as simply here for us in favor of the recognition that they also live 'for themselves' and for God."[26]

Since Linzey kicked off the conversation in the mid-1970s, interest in the ethical treatment of animals has grown among Christian scholars and the larger Christian community. Matthew Scully, a conservative Catholic who wrote speeches for President George W. Bush, had a powerful impact on Christians and non-Christians alike with his book *Dominion: The Power of Man, the Suffering of Animals, and the Call to Mercy.*[27] Scully argues against the hypocritical use of the dominionist mandate to justify cruelty to animals and offers numerous examples of how some people misuse Christian teachings to justify their egregious behavior, including trophy hunters and those who've grown wealthy from factory farming.

Another contemporary Christian leader who has been outspoken in his advocacy for animals is Desmond Tutu, the South African Anglican bishop and theologian who won the Nobel Peace Prize in 1984 for his role in the nonviolent campaign to end apartheid in South Africa. Tutu was a social- and racial-justice advocate, but he was also an animal- and earth-justice advocate. In the foreword to the *Global Guide to Animal Protection* published in 2023, Tutu wrote:

> I have seen first-hand how injustice gets overlooked when the victims are powerless or vulnerable, when they have no one to speak up for them and no means of representing themselves to a higher authority. Animals are in precisely that position. Unless we are mindful of their interests and speak out loudly on their behalf, abuse and cruelty go unchallenged. It is a kind of theological folly to suppose that God has made the entire world just for human beings, or to suppose that God is interested in only one of the millions of species that inhabit God's good earth. . . . Our dominion over animals is not supposed to be despotism. We are made in the image of God, yes, but God—in whose image we are made—is holy, loving, and just. We do not honour God by abusing other sentient creatures. If it is true that we are the most exalted species in creation, it is equally true that we can be the most debased and sinful. This realization should give us pause. There is something Christ-like about caring for suffering creatures, whether they are humans or animals.[28]

Tutu goes on to assert that "churches should lead the way by making clear that all forms of cruelty—to other animals as well as human beings—is an affront to civilized living and a sin before God."[29]

So what constitutes good stewardship and what does not? For many Christians, the answer to this question lies with a familiar query: What would Jesus do? Jesus taught that love is the most important quality for humankind, directly challenging the notion that rational thought is our most valuable asset. René Descartes is famous for declaring, "I think, therefore I am." But Presbyterian minister William Sloane Coffin challenges this notion: "*Cogito ergo sum*: 'I think, therefore I am?' Nonsense. *Amo ergo sum*: 'I love, therefore I am.'"[30]

Notably, historical research into the lives of Jesus and his followers supports the position that they were deeply concerned with animal suffering and oppression. In *Disciples*, theologian Keith Akers asserts that early sacred writings show that Jesus and his followers were part of a movement known as Jewish Christianity. The movement was pacifist and predated Jesus, but Jesus was eventually chosen as its leader because of his commitment to nonviolence. As a group, the Jewish Christians eschewed violence of all kinds and followed a vegetarian lifestyle. They believed the path to salvation lay in the compassionate treatment of God's creation and full immersion baptism, and they rejected the Mosaic law in effect at that time that required animal sacrifice during Passover, a practice they abhorred. As Akers writes, "Jewish Christianity saw the practice of animal sacrifice in the temple as a bloody and barbaric business. The chief business of the ancient temple was accepting the offerings of slaughtered animals. It was more like a butcher shop than a place of worship. For Jewish Christianity, Jesus gave his life when he disrupted the temple business during Passover week. Instead of animal sacrifice, they practiced an alternative ritual, baptism in flowing water, and were vegetarians."[31]

In the centuries that followed the death of Christ, many prominent religious orders adopted a plant-based diet, including the Benedictines, Franciscans, Carthusians, Cistercians, and Trappists, all of which flourished in the Middle Ages. In recent decades, some Christians have adopted a vegetarian or plant-based diet out of concern for the cruelty of the food animal industry. One organization, the Christian Vegetarian Association (christianveg.org), offers resources and theological guidance to its members, claiming that "a plant-based diet helps preserve our health and serves God by avoiding the animal cruelty, environmental damage, and human misery associated with factory farms."[32] Similarly, CreatureKind (becreaturekind.org) promotes a more loving relationship with all of God's creation. Launched in January 2016 by Christian theologians David Clough and Sarah Withrow King, this nonprofit provides "education and support to Christian leaders to change the way animals are viewed by Christians, and to encourage Christians to recognize faith-based reasons for caring about the well-being of fellow animal creatures used for food, and to take practical action in response."[33] According to King, "From Genesis to Revelation, and from the early church to the present day, there are vivid examples of God's—and the church's—love of, care for, and delight in animal creatures."[34]

The concern among Christians for the plight of nonhuman animals extends to all of nature. Over the last fifty years, many Christian churches have embraced EarthCare Missions and incorporated the Season of Creation into their liturgical calendars to raise awareness among congregants about the toll of human progress on the earth and to call on them to pray and engage in community events that deepen their relationship with God, their neighbors, animals, and the earth itself. The Season of Creation traditionally begins on September 1, the World Day of Prayer for the Care of Creation, and ends on October 4, the Feast of St. Francis of Assisi, the Catholic patron saint of animals.

These are encouraging developments. Yet the evolving beliefs about animals described here are not mainstream. Modern-day Christians might describe themselves as animal lovers, but relatively few appear to consider themselves to be animal advocates, and only a tiny proportion follow a plant-based diet because of ethical concerns about animals. As I've said, what constitutes responsible stewardship is still being debated in Christian circles and probably always will be.

So what does the future hold for animals, spirituality, and our religious lives? Will more places of worship adopt a more animal- and Earth-friendly mindset? Only time will tell, but the strictly anthropocentric worldview that has long characterized the West's religious institutions appears to be shifting. My worry is that the long-standing ideology of human exceptionalism will continue to be used as a barricade against a more inclusive vision of the cosmos. My hope is that more people of faith—and I mean *all* faiths, not just Christianity—will embrace a more holistic interpretation of sacred teachings about animals, the natural world, and the interconnection of all living creatures. In the absence of any other meaningful ethical framework to guide our conduct toward other life-forms, such teachings can help us honor the loss of our animal family members just as we honor the loss of our human family members. This would be a solid first step in the right direction for pet keepers and their families and, in my view, for society as a whole.

Notably, the shift in beliefs about animals taking place in religious circles is also taking place in the world of science. As we'll see in the next chapter, scientific understandings of animal intelligence, emotions, and physiology have undergone a sea-change in the last century. Because our world is dominated by science, these changes will likely have a far-reaching impact on the evolving relationship between humans and other animals.

## CHAPTER 9

# The New Animal Science

In 1995 University of Colorado medical student Safia Rubaii refused to perform a compulsory experiment in her physiology course that required her to give a lethal injection to an anesthetized dog. Because of her refusal, she failed her course. She sued the university, claiming she was forced to retake physiology at another university where animals were not harmed during medical training. When upholding Rubaii's legal claims, the court required the University of Colorado to provide alternative training methods to students who might request them in the future, and "dog labs," as they are commonly known, have since been replaced at the University of Colorado Medical School with humane alternatives[1]

Veterinarian Jennifer Kissinger had a similar experience at Ohio State University's veterinary college in the early 1990s when she refused to participate in surgical procedures in which healthy animals were killed. When she was expelled, Kissinger sued the school and was eventually permitted to reenter the program and use substitutes for the live-animal labs. "Even though the animals that were being used were due to be euthanized anyway, I still felt it was unethical," she says. "Human doctors don't kill homeless people, and it seems the height of hypocrisy to allow vets to do the same thing."[2]

An increasing number of medical schools, veterinary colleges, and other scientific and medical institutions have abandoned traditional training methods that use living, healthy animals in favor of more humane methods. To date, however, such practices are still widespread. At present, only six of the thirty-seven veterinary colleges accredited by the American Veterinary Medical Association (AVMA) in the US and Canada have eliminated the use of live animals in veterinary training; the remainder use a combination of alternative techniques in addition to small and large animals.[3] In 2024, the American Association of Veterinary Medical Colleges (AAVMC) published guidelines for the use of living animals in veterinary education that are intended to "contribute to progress in this area by promoting effective animal alternatives, supporting animal welfare and animal ethics, and the safety of veterinary students and the animals with which they learn."[4]

For people who believe it's morally wrong to end the life of a healthy animal, these are welcome developments. As with many of the other issues discussed in this book, the belief that it's ethically acceptable to sacrifice the lives of healthy animals in the name of human progress has long been questioned by lay people and scientists alike. Yet, until quite recently, any researcher, scientist, or clinician who challenged this perspective was ridiculed and ostracized by their fellow scientists. Similarly, until quite recently, any researcher, scientist, or clinician who claimed that animals are emotional and intelligent was also ridiculed and ostracized.

The scientific world long ago stripped away the supernatural summit of Aristotle's Great Chain of Being. Yet many scientists and scholars continue to view the living world hierarchically, and most place humans at the top of this hierarchy. As noted by animal ethicist Paul Waldau, "The vast majority of scholarship in the Western intellectual tradition has gone forward on the assumption that humans are the only animals with intellectual ability, emotions, social complexity, and personality development."[5] To this day, animals are used in scientific testing as if they are mindless, unfeeling machines. Animal welfare laws were introduced in the US in the 1960s to improve the lives of animals in laboratory testing. Yet such laws appear to be only marginally effective and are not consistently enforced. Rats, mice, and birds—the species used most frequently in laboratories—have been excluded from the US's Animal Welfare Act solely because the organizations that use these animals insist it would be too expensive to discontinue their use. Each year an estimated seventy-one million animals of varying species are used worldwide for product testing, predominantly in the medical, cosmetic, and chemical industries.[6] The US tops the list with an estimated twenty million test animals in 2020, followed by China with sixteen million animals. This includes dogs, cats, and other species commonly kept as pets in the West.

In the last thirty years, however, new perspectives about animals have gained strength in the scientific community, and this shift is likely to have a profound impact on how animals are used as test subjects. The more we learn about the complex inner lives of animals and appreciate their unique skills and abilities, the more difficult it may become to treat them as unfeeling objects. HAS scholar and author Margo DeMello commented on this dynamic when she wrote, "Animals have long served as objects of study—in biology, zoology, medical science, anthropology, and the like—but were rarely considered to be more than that, and were even more rarely considered to be 'subjects of a life' rather than objects of study. . . . [But when] we grant that animals have subjectivity, including their own interests, wants, and desires, it becomes more difficult to justify many of the practices that humans engage in with animals, such as meat consumption or medical experimentation."[7]

When René Descartes declared in 1641 that animals are complex machines that lack emotions, intelligence, or the ability to experience pain, the stage was set for a scientific world that regarded animals solely as objects of study with little concern for their well-being. But over the centuries, especially in the last fifty years, this perspective gradually shifted as pioneering scientists revealed that many of our fellow creatures are much more like us than we'd previously acknowledged. As noted in the introduction, our relationship with animals in Western society is in the midst of a vast paradigm shift, and scientists are having a huge impact on this phenomenon. Scientists are greatly respected in our increasingly secular society, so when accomplished, well-respected scientists speak out, we're likely to listen. They're like the new Noahs of our age, helping us understand the animals in our midst and see them with new eyes.

## From Darwin to Goodall

The first major challenge to the traditional scientific view of animals came in 1836 when the English naturalist Charles Darwin set sail on the scientific survey ship the HMS Beagle. The ship traveled around the tip of South America before continuing north to the coast of Chile and, finally, to the Galapagos Islands off the western coast of Ecuador. The voyage took five years, and by 1838 Darwin was beginning to formulate his insights into a comprehensive theory about the shared evolution of all living creatures. Twenty years later, Darwin compiled his controversial ideas in the groundbreaking book, *On the Origin of Species,* which offered compelling empirical evidence that living creatures evolve over time as they adapt to their environment.[8]

But Darwin wasn't done. A bigger bombshell came twelve years later in 1871 when he published *The Descent of Man,* followed in 1872 by *The Expression of the Emotions in Man and Animals.*[9] Darwin asserted that, because they had a common ancestry, humans and some animals, especially the great apes, share many anatomical characteristics and many cognitive and emotional capacities as well. "There is no fundamental difference between man and the higher animals in their mental faculties," Darwin wrote.[10] Rather, the difference between humans and other animals is one of degree, not of kind, and all complex creatures lie somewhere on a continuum of intelligence and emotional complexity. "Darwin proved that not only are humans and all other animals related but also that we together feel pain, share emotions, and possess memory, reason, and imagination," writes HAS scholar Margo DeMello. "Rather than seeing humans and animals as categorically different, Darwin showed that all animals, including humans, share a continuum of mental and emotional capacities."[11]

Darwin's work challenged the widespread belief in Western society that people are the pinnacle of creation, far superior to all other forms of life. As you might expect, his work was met with a ferocious backlash. Christian leaders were outraged that Darwin had challenged Christian doctrine, claiming he had refuted the word of God. Even in scientific circles, Darwin's ideas were regarded with skepticism, and many of his fellow scientists thought his conclusions too radical. Resistance to Darwin's ideas was so strong that it would take nearly a hundred years before evolutionary theory was widely accepted in Western society, and it is still rejected by people who hold a literal interpretation of the Christian creation story.

Darwin's evolutionary theory eventually gained acceptance in the scientific establishment because his research was so thorough and his claims empirically irrefutable. Natural selection has long been the scientific standard for framing the incredible diversity of species that inhabit this planet and the interconnectedness of all forms of life. Yet Darwin's ideas about the continuity between human and animal cognition and emotions continued to face fierce resistance in the scientific world throughout most of the twentieth century. Researchers in a variety of fields, from zoology and biology to comparative psychology, have drawn a hard line between the cognitive abilities and emotional experiences of human and nonhuman animals. Renowned primatologist Frans de Waal, who studied primates both in the lab and in the wild beginning in the 1970s, summarizes this deeply entrenched perspective in the following passage from the book *Are We Smart Enough to Realize How Smart Animals Are?*:

For most of the last century, science was overly cautious

and skeptical about the intelligence of animals. Attributing intentions and emotions to animals was seen as naïve 'folk' nonsense. We, the scientists, knew better! . . . The two dominant schools of thought viewed animals as either stimulus-response machines out to obtain rewards and avoid punishment or as robots genetically endowed with useful instincts. While each school fought the other and deemed it too narrow, they shared a fundamentally mechanistic outlook: there was no need to worry about the internal lives of animals, and anyone who did was anthropomorphic, romantic, or unscientific.[12]

The belief that animal behavior is driven solely by biological instincts has been so pervasive in the West's scientific circles that it has spread into disciplines only indirectly related to the study of animals. In fact, the belief that humans are innately superior to other animals may be more pervasive in the humanities than in the hard sciences of biology and zoology. According to de Waal, many humanities scholars assume that "evolution stopped at the human head. This idea remains prevalent in much of the social sciences, philosophy, and the humanities. It views our minds as so original that there is no point comparing it to other minds except to confirm its exceptional status."[13]

de Waal refers to this perspective as *neocreationism*, and this belief appears to be common among humanities scholars. Consider, for example, the writings of cultural anthropologist Ernest Becker, whose theory of death anxiety was discussed in chapter 3. Although Becker demonstrates an astute and nuanced understanding of the human animal, he also held a mainstream view of nonhuman animals, writing that animal instincts may be understood as "a programmed perception that calls into play a programmed reaction," and that "animals live in a tiny world, a sliver of reality, one neuron-chemical program that keeps them walking behind their nose and shuts out everything else."[14] Other humanities scholars go even further. Stephen Budiansky, an American historian, asserts that animals are "programmed to 'mimic' pain and enjoyment alike" and that for animals, "Sentience is not sentience, and pain isn't even pain. . . . Consciousness is a wonderful gift and a wonderful curse that, all the evidence suggests, is not in the realm of the sentient experience of other creatures."[15]

As I said, such perspectives dominated the academic world for most of the twentieth century. Yet there were early detractors. One of the most influential scientists who challenged the notion that animals are inherently inferior to people was Baltic-German zoologist Jakob von Uexküll. In 1909 von Uexküll introduced the concept of *Umwelt* to the scientific world.[16] *Umwelt* comes from the German word for environment, but Uexküll used the term specifically to denote an animal's perceptual world. Uexküll equated *Umwelt* to a house with many windows that a creature uses to navigate the world. Every living being, including humans, has a unique house, or a set of sensory strengths and weaknesses. Notably, Uexküll did not position the human *Umwelt* as superior to that of other animals, as noted by science writer Ed Yong:

> Unlike many of his contemporaries, Uexküll saw animals not as mere machines but as sentient entities, whose inner worlds not only existed but were worth contemplating. Uexküll didn't exalt the inner worlds of humans over those of other species. Rather, he treated the *Umwelt* concept as a unifying and leveling force. The human's house might be bigger than the tick's, with more windows overlooking a wider garden, but we are still stuck inside one, looking out. Our *Umwelt* is still limited; it just doesn't feel that way. To us, it feels all-encompassing. It is all that we know, and so we easily mistake it for all there is to know. This is an illusion, and one that every animal shares.[17]

When we consider the remarkable capabilities of some creatures, it becomes much less straightforward to position humans at the top of Aristotle's Great Chain of Being. What do we make of sharks and platypuses who can sense electrical fields that we cannot? Birds and sea turtles who can detect magnetic fields and navigate the globe guided by these fields? Rodents who communicate with ultrasonic calls, and elephants and whales who communicate by infrasonic sounds? Yes, we have many qualities that other animals may lack, but those abilities do not necessarily equate to superiority. Rather, they are evidence of the fantastic diversity of life on this planet.

The work of Darwin and other scientists who've followed in his footsteps has shown that the living world does not resemble a hierarchical ladder but a dense, branching tree. Evolution does not always equate to progress, such that one life-form can be judged superior to another. "We are not the culmination of all these 'lesser' beings," observes science writer Virginia Morell in the book *Animal Wise*. "They are not lesser, and we are not the pinnacle of evolution. We are not more highly evolved—either physically or mentally—than our closest genetic ancestor, the chimpanzee. . . . Evolution is not linear. It is divergent."[18]

Another significant turning point in the prevailing scientific paradigm about animals came in 1965 when primatologist Jane Goodall appeared in living rooms worldwide as the star of the film *Miss Goodall and the Wild Chimpanzees*. Produced by the National Geographic Society, the film documented her work studying chimpanzees in the dense forests of what is now Tanzania. The public fell in love with Goodall and was touched by intimate scenes of the chimps grooming each other and caring for their babies. One of the chimps Goodall studied was a big male who she'd named David Greybeard, who was filmed using a stick to fish termites out of a mound. This was a groundbreaking discovery because the use of tools was believed to be an exclusively human capability.

When Goodall died in late 2025, she was widely considered the world's foremost chimpanzee expert who revolutionized our understanding of animals, broke barriers for women in science, and became a global icon for environmental advocacy. What most people don't realize is that her reception in the male-dominated world of science at the beginning of her sixty-year career was anything but stellar. To begin with, Goodall was not a trained scientist when she first began studying Tanzania's chimps. She was working as a secretary and typist for the famed paleoanthropologist Louis S. B. Leakey when she jumped at the opportunity to study the chimps in Tanzania. In the field, she recorded what she saw as carefully and honestly as she could. A year after she began working under Leakey's tutelage, he arranged for her to return to England to work toward her PhD in ethology at Cambridge University. Many years later, Goodall reflected on that event, writing that at Cambridge, "I was criticized for my lack of scientific method, for naming the chimpanzees rather than assigning each a number, for 'giving' them personalities, and for maintaining they had minds and emotions. For these, I was told sternly, were attributes reserved for the human animal. I was even reprimanded for referring to a male chimpanzee as 'he' and a female as 'she': Didn't I know that 'it' was the correct way to refer to an animal?"[19]

Goodall was shocked by this response, but she was also determined to continue her pioneering work with the chimps. With Leakey's blessing, she continued to give them names and record their behavior, including her perceptions about their personalities and emotional lives. Eventually, she realized that some animal scientists, "along with many philosophers and theologians, argued that personality, mind, and emotions were uniquely human attributes and that the behavior of nonhuman animals was for the most part merely a response to some environmental social stimulus. But I could not accept this—it absolutely contradicted all I had learned during my years with [my dog] Rusty and my experiences with the chimpanzees."[20]

## A Sea Change in Animal Science

By the mid-1970s, a radically different perspective about animal minds and emotions that was in keeping with Goodall's novel approach to studying chimps had begun to gain ground in scientific circles. Known as *cognitive ethology*, this new branch of animal studies was formally introduced by bat researcher Donald R. Griffin in 1976 with the publication of the controversial book *The Question of Animal Awareness*.[21] Griffin and some of his fellow scientists were uncomfortable with the narrow view of animals espoused by the scientific establishment. They embraced Darwin's belief that humans and other animals share a continuum of emotions and intelligence. In defending this position, Griffin pointed to a central tenet of experimental science: an absence of evidence is not evidence of absence.[22] The fact that we've struggled to find a scientifically valid or empirically rigorous way to prove that animals think and feel doesn't mean that they don't. As noted by primatologist de Waal, "There are many ways to process, organize, and spread information. And it is only recently that science has become open-minded enough to treat all these different methods with wonder and amazement rather than dismissal and denial. . . . We love to compare and contrast animal and human intelligence, taking ourselves as the touchstone. [But] this is an outdated way of putting it."[23]

Today, cognitive ethology is defined as "the comparative, evolutionary, and ecological study of animal minds. It focuses on how animals think and what they feel, and this includes their emotions, beliefs, reasoning, information processing, consciousness, and self-awareness."[24] Cognitive ethologists claim that our limited and erroneous understanding of animals' inner lives is due, in part, to an unintentional but unquestioned bias against animals. It's also just bad science, because the experiments scientists created to study animals were poorly constructed. For most of the past century, for example, wild animals were captured and brought into laboratories. Caged and separated from their natural habitats and social groups, these animals were subjected to a wide range of experiments, both physiological and psychological. In these artificial conditions, their behavior was quite different from what it would be in their normal habitat. Given such stressful conditions, it's no wonder that many lab animals failed miserably at the tasks they were given to measure their intelligence.

It's also important to note that traditional methods for testing animal intelligence and emotions were ill-suited to the species being studied. Lab animals were often required to manipulate objects their bodies were not designed to handle or to complete tasks they had no interest in. Intelligence was defined solely by human standards, and a particular species' *Umwelt* was ignored. On this issue, de Waal offers the following humorous observation:

> It seems highly unfair to ask if a squirrel can count to ten if counting is not really what a squirrel's life is about. The squirrel is very good at retrieving hidden nuts, though, and some birds are absolute experts. The Clark's nutcracker, in the fall, stores more than twenty thousand pine nuts, in hundreds of different locations distributed over many square miles; then in winter and spring it manages to recover the majority of them. That we can't compete with squirrels and nutcrackers on this task—I even forget where I parked my car—is irrelevant, since our species does not need this kind of memory for survival the way forest animals braving a freezing winter do.[25]

In the early 2000s, a growing number of scientists began challenging the unquestioned assumptions about animals that have long characterized the field. According to psychologist and researcher Hal Herzog, who conducted tests on the personalities of snakes in the 1980s, "At that time the idea that animals had personalities was taboo among animal behavior researchers."[26] Over the past two decades, however, the number of research papers on animal personality jumped from zero in 1990 to more than 900 in 2020.[27] This research has shown that many species of animals share the same emotions as people and also display many of the same personality traits, including openness to new experiences, conscientiousness, extroversion-introversion, agreeableness, and neuroticism/anxiety.

In July 2012, an international group of leading scientists gathered at Cambridge University in England to discuss animal consciousness. The group released the Cambridge Declaration on Consciousness, confirming that "nonhuman animals have the neuroanatomical, neurochemical, and neurophysiological substrates of conscious states along with the capacity to exhibit intentional behaviors. Consequently, the weight of evidence indicates that humans are not unique in possessing the neurological substrates that generate consciousness. Nonhuman animals, including all mammals and birds, and many other creatures, including octopuses, also possess these neurological substrates."[28] Given these physiological similarities, it's illogical to assume that other animals don't share many of the same cognitive and emotional experiences previously thought to be the sole domain of human beings. This is not to say that animals experience the world in precisely the same way as people, but as Darwin pointed out, whatever differences exist are a matter of degree, not of kind. "If we look hard enough, we can find the roots of our own intelligence and emotions in other animals," writes one animal scientist. "The similarities and contrasts among species are nuances or shades of gray, not stark black and white differences."[29]

An increasing proportion of scientists who study animals have adopted the more open-minded perspective introduced by cognitive ethologists. One of the most influential is Marc Bekoff, a professor emeritus of ecology and evolutionary biology at the University of Colorado Boulder. Bekoff spent years studying coyotes in the field. Like Goodall, with whom he's co-authored numerous books and scholarly articles, Bekoff has withstood sharp criticism from other scientists throughout his career because of his insistence that highly social animals like wolves not only possess complex emotions but also demonstrate moral behavior. Some of this criticism was scientifically oriented as his peers questioned his methods and his findings. But much of it was personal in nature and not grounded in science at all.

Despite the rejection he's experienced among many of his scientific peers, Bekoff maintains that research clearly shows that the scientific world has consistently underestimated animals' emotions. "It's bad biology to argue against the existence of animal emotions," Bekoff writes. "Scientific research in evolutionary biology, cognitive ethology, and social neuroscience supports the view that numerous and diverse animals have rich and deep emotional lives. Emotions have evolved as adaptions in numerous species, and they serve as a social glue to bond animals with one another. . . . Emotions, empathy, and knowing right from wrong are keys to survival, without which animals—both human and nonhuman—would perish."[30]

Consider, for example, the issue of *anthropomorphism*, a term that refers to the belief that any humanlike emotion or personality trait we ascribe to an animal is merely the result of our own mental or emotional projections. According to this idea, if you look at your dog and believe you see love in his eyes when he gazes back at you, you're anthropomorphizing his behavior because you cannot empirically prove that your dog loves you. Similarly, if you describe your cat as curious or bold, then you're merely projecting your own curiosity and boldness onto your cat. But Bekoff insists that "personal truths are valid; if they are acknowledged and accounted for, they don't need to compromise objectivity."[31]

Anthropomorphism has long been considered a derogatory word in scientific circles and has been used as a blanket response to any claim about animal intelligence and emotions. Bekoff acknowledges that our inclination to ascribe emotions to animals is sometimes anthropomorphic, but this does not mean that our judgments about an animal's emotions are imagined or inaccurate. "It is sometimes easier to see and understand emotions in animals than in humans because animals do not filter their emotions," he writes. "What they feel is clearly written on their faces, made public by their tails, ears, and odors, and displayed by their actions. Animal emotions are raw and out there for all to see, hear, smell, and feel. . . . It is surprisingly easy to recognize basic or primary emotions in animals."[32]

Any pet keeper can tell you that animals are highly emotional. In fact, a 2015 survey found that 94 percent of pet keepers said that their companion animal had humanlike personality traits, such as being emotionally sensitive, outgoing, inquisitive, stubborn, and laid back.[33] They also communicate with us and with each other, primarily through body language. When a cat raises her tail, for example, it generally indicates that she is happy and feels good about the world, whereas flattened ears and a lowered tail indicate that she is feeling angry or upset. Among dogs, tail wagging is often interpreted as a sign of happiness, but it is actually a sign of arousal and can signal different emotions depending on its direction. A helicopter tail, as when a dog's tail spins in a circle, typically signals intense happiness, while a tail wagged to the left probably indicates that the dog is feeling something negative.[34]

The eyes of highly social creatures like dogs, cats, wolves, apes, and humans are particularly important for communication, both within and between species. Studies have confirmed the powerful and mysterious way in which the eyes serve as a portal into animals' inner lives.[35] Pet keepers often refer to this magical interchange as "eye talk," and they take great pleasure in gazing into their animal's eyes. Chemically speaking, the pleasure we experience in those moments is related to oxytocin, known as the love hormone, which floods the bodies of both people and pets when they stare into each other's eyes.[36]

Although it has taken centuries, the scientific community is beginning to offer a much more nuanced and accurate understanding of the animals in our midst. Science writer Virginia Morell writes that leading scientists no longer ask *if* animals think and feel but *how* and *what* they think and feel. They are confirming what many pet keepers understand intuitively about their animal companions:

> Animals have minds. They have brains, and use them, as we
> do: for experiencing the world, for thinking and feeling, and
> for solving the problems of life every creature faces. Like us,
> they have personalities, moods, and emotions; they laugh and
> they play. Some show grief and empathy and are self-aware

and very likely conscious of their actions and intents. Not so long ago, I would have hedged these statements, because the prevailing notion held that animals are more like zombies or robotic machines, capable of responding with only simple, reflexive behaviors. And indeed there are still researchers who insist that animals are moving through life like the half dead, but they're so . . . 1950s. They've been left behind as a flood of new research from biologists, animal behaviorists, evolutionary and ecological biologists, comparative psychologists, cognitive ethologists, and neuroscientists sweeps away old ideas that block the exploration of animal minds.[37]

In thousands of studies in a variety of academic disciplines, scientists have discovered that animals are a lot more like humans than we've been led to believe. Many wild animals live in complex social communities defined by cooperation, empathy, dominance, and cruelty, much like humans. Donkeys have a sense of humor and like to play tricks on their human and animal companions. Elephants and foxes grieve the loss of their fellows and sometimes bury their dead. Hens love to play. Rats and cows engage in altruistic behavior. Almost all birds are monogamous, and many mate for life. Crows and chimpanzees use tools and can project the results of their actions, like a chess player. Such insights are emerging rapidly in the scientific literature, as well as in books and websites aimed at a lay audience, and they have the potential to radically change the way we think about and interact with animals.

## Listening to Our Hearts

Although our understanding of animals has changed greatly in the last fifty years, the ethical norms that guide our interactions with our fellow creatures continue to rest on the unquestioned belief that human needs outweigh those of all other living beings. Today, as in the past, economic interests heavily influence what constitutes the acceptable treatment of animals. As noted by Wayne Purcell, former president of the Humane Society of the United States, "Especially within the last two hundred years, we've come to apply an industrial mind-set to the use of animals, too often viewing them as if they were nothing but articles of commerce and the raw material of science, agriculture, and wildlife management. Here, as in other pursuits, human ingenuity has a way of outrunning human conscience, and some things we do only because we can—forgetting to ask whether we should."[38]

The point is that science without ethics can be a dangerous thing. New understandings of animals as thinking, feeling beings won't change the status quo unless we're willing to set ethical limits on how we study animals and engage with them in our everyday lives. This entails reflecting critically on our personal biases and, when necessary, challenging the institutions that seek to preserve the status quo. Science, like religion, resists change. Although we're taught that science is a purely objective endeavor, this is a misrepresentation of what scientific research actually entails. Science is most accurately understood as an ongoing debate about the world, and we're continuously discovering that we still have a great deal to learn about this amazing, complex world and its diverse life-forms.

It's also important to acknowledge that every scientist is socially conditioned by their culture and inevitably bring their personal beliefs to their work. If a researcher hasn't honestly examined their own assumptions about the world, then their personal biases inevitably shape the way they create their research projects and interpret their data. Ultimately, personal bias is inescapable, and one scientist's bias can have a knock-on effect on the entire scientific community, especially if their bias is commonplace. Scientists have long insisted that animals are inherently inferior to humans, and decades of research across all academic disciplines reflect this bias. As observed by philosopher and animal rights pioneer Tom Regan, "Because we have viewed other animals through the myopic lens of our self-importance, we have misperceived who and what they are. Because we have repeated our ignorance, one to the other, we have mistaken it for knowledge."[39]

At the beginning of this chapter, I shared the stories of medical student Safia Rubaii and veterinary student Jennifer Kissinger, who successfully sued their universities for forcing them to end the lives of healthy animals in their studies. It took great fortitude and moral courage for these students to challenge authority and weather the social ostracism that people who question institutional power almost always suffer. Similarly, the late Jane Goodall showed moral courage when she challenged the scientific protocol that prohibited scientists from naming the animals they studied, and Marc Bekoff demonstrated moral courage in refusing to comply with his peers' prevailing attitude that animals lack minds and feelings.

In *The Emotional Lives of Animals*, Bekoff shared the precise moment when he realized he could no longer contribute as a scientist to animal suffering. As a graduate student, he participated in a study that required him to kill cats for his research. He said that he had secretly named one of those cats Speedo, and on the day he was supposed to end Speedo's life, the cat looked directly at him and held his gaze. "As I picked him up, he looked at me and asked, 'Why me?'" Bekoff wrote. "Tears came to my eyes. He wouldn't break his piercing stare. Though I followed through with what I was supposed to do and killed him, it broke my heart to do so. To this day, I remember his unwavering eyes—they told the whole story of the interminable pain and indignity he had endured. Others in the program tried to reassure me that it was all worth it, but I never recovered from that experience. So I left the program and entered another one in which naming was not only permitted but actively encouraged, and I resolved not to conduct research that involved intentionally inflicting pain or causing the death of another being."[40]

Like Rubaii, Kissinger, Goodall, and many others, Bekoff listened to his heart, and his heart spoke louder than the powerful voices of his research peers, the institution that was funding his research, and society as a whole. He eventually emerged as an outspoken advocate for animals in the world of animal science, insisting that "solid science can easily be done with ethics and compassion. There's nothing wrong with compassionate or sentimental science or scientists. Studies of animal thought, emotions, and self-awareness, as well as behavioral ecology and conservation biology, can all be compassionate as well as scientifically rigorous. Science and the ethical treatment of animals aren't incompatible. We can do solid science with an open mind and a big heart."[41]

Pet keepers are also listening to their hearts, and, collectively, people who've embraced animals as cherished family members have a significant role to play in the growing animal advocacy movement. Because of their sheer numbers, pet keepers in the US and other pet-loving countries can substantively change how we think about animals. Is it possible that pets could be our ambassadors to a new cultural paradigm, one that sees animals as kin and fellow travelers? I hope so, and as we'll see in the next chapter, there's solid evidence that pets and their human guardians are having a positive influence on the evolution of the human-animal bond.

# Discussion Questions

1. In your own words, define what the word *soul* means to you. Next, define your beliefs about animals and the concept of the soul. Do you believe animals have souls? Why or why not?

2. In chapter 8, we learned that some observers believe Cartesian dualism has had a harmful impact on Western society because we've tended to denigrate the physical aspects of our lives while elevating the spiritual. What are your thoughts on this idea? For example, how do you believe dualistic thinking has impacted our relationships with our pets?

3. Chapter 8 also noted that most Christians believe they must be good stewards of God's creation. What does "good stewardship" mean to you? Be specific in your answer.

4. Chapter 9 traced the ongoing changes in how scientists view and study animals in Western society. Why do you think scientists and other scholars have been slow to change their perspective about animals?

5. How do you define animal intelligence? What have you observed in your own pets or learned in your work or studies about this topic?

6. What impact do you think new scientific understandings of animals will have on the lives of animals in the future?

# For the Love of Our Pets

## CHAPTER 10

# Across the Rainbow Bridge

In 1994 a "Dear Abby" reader in Grand Rapids, Michigan, sent a copy of a poem about animals and the afterlife that they'd received from the Humane Society to the popular advice column. Titled "The Rainbow Bridge," the poem was not attributed, but Abby printed it anyway. Since then, the poem has been distributed far and wide: across the internet, in printed pamphlets distributed by animal rescue organizations and veterinarians, in pet loss books, and on markers in pet cemeteries. It has provided solace to thousands, if not millions, of grieving people.

The origin of "The Rainbow Bridge Poem" was disputed for years until researcher Paul Koudounaris tracked down the anonymous author in 2022 while writing a book on the history of pet cemeteries. The poem was written in 1959 by Edna Clyne-Rekhy, a Scottish artist, shortly after the loss of her dog Major.[1] Edna was only nineteen when she penned the poem, but she was able to produce her original handwritten version, penciled on a piece of notebook paper that she had tucked away as a keepsake for more than sixty years. "While she hadn't preconceived any of it, it was there, words longing to be heard," Koudounaris wrote about his interview with Edna. "She remembers it being a warm and wonderful feeling, like Major himself was guiding her in what to write."[2]

"The Rainbow Bridge" has an undeniably spiritual quality. Life for the animals on the bridge is eternally happy and carefree. The hills and meadows where the animals romp and play are reminiscent of the lush and beautiful garden of Eden. The bridge serves as a temporary limbo for pets who predecease their keepers, spanning the interstice between this world and heaven. The poem's popularity can be attributed in part to the fact that it provides an alternative way for pets to be reunited with their human companion and thereby gain passage into heaven, sidestepping the uncertainty about animal afterlife in mainline Christianity. As Koudounaris observes, the poem "serves as a kind of theological plug in. As an elastic concept that can be applied to any faith, it provides a clearly expressed means for us to reunite with our pets in the afterlife. In so doing, it gives hope where a person may have been previously acculturated to believe there was none. . . . [It's] most influential pieces of mourning literature ever written."[3]

Today, "The Rainbow Bridge" poem is ubiquitous in the pet-keeping world. It's a beautiful tribute to a beloved pet and represents a creative response to a difficult loss. It also highlights that when our institutions fail to meet our needs, we often find creative ways to meet them ourselves, and these creative responses can have a profound impact on the world.

In the absence of support from their faith communities, pet keepers have embraced what is essentially a separate but not quite equal system of death rites for their pets. They've begun to carve out sacred spaces, both physical and virtual, where the lives of their animals can be celebrated and their passing marked with familiar and comforting rituals that have long been reserved for people. Today, people grieving a pet can choose from a growing selection of pet loss books, online forums, and emergency hotlines. Flower arrangements and sympathy cards crafted specifically for pet loss are now available, and pet keepers can choose from a wide variety of pet shrines, tombstones, and other products that help them memorialize their animals. It's even possible to have your pet's ashes turned into a pendant that will keep your animal literally next to your heart. These are all encouraging signs that pet loss is emerging as a serious topic in our society.

People who are sharing their pet passion with the world are emerging as a formidable force in contemporary Western Society. It's likely their voices will only grow louder as they seek the support they need, lending truth to the old saying that where there is a will, there is a way.

## The Obit Page

Though not generally religious in focus, obituaries published in local newspapers and online are considered unofficial public records—a place where we can reliably mark the passing of a loved one, affirm our familial ties, and celebrate the deceased's accomplishments and contributions to the community.

Some people mention pets in human obits as surviving family members, but dedicated obits for pets are rarely allowed to appear side by side with those for humans. This unwritten rule can be disenfranchising for pet keepers. When an acquaintance of mine submitted an obituary about a former military service dog to her local newspaper, she was refused. Her dog's obit was finally accepted after she tweaked the language to obscure the deceased's identity as a dog. And, of course, she didn't send a photo.

Another example of this phenomenon concerns a dog named Bear, a black lab who was apparently a fixture on the streets of his small Iowa town. His obit appeared in the *Iowa City Press-Citizen* alongside those for people. An article on the National Public Radio website chronicled the conflict that erupted in response to Bear's obit. "Bear, who frequently walked along, and napped on, the town streets, had been known to many locals," the article read. "Even so, that brief obituary became the cause of bitter debate in the community. Especially offended was a woman whose sister-in-law's obituary had appeared on the same page as Bear's. Discord erupted in the town as words like 'distasteful' and 'disrespectful' were hurled around to describe Bear's printed memorial."[4]

Another touching dedication was penned for a cat named Harlequin, or Harley for short. It was written by Susan Palwick, who is a friend, a talented and successful fantasy writer, a board-certified chaplain (she loves the emergency department), a graduate of my veterinary chaplaincy course, a social worker, a former English professor, and, perhaps most important of all, a cat lover. Susan wrote her tribute to Harley in the form of a traditional obituary, like the kind you find in your local newspaper. It's a humorous remembrance that reflects the joy and laughter Harley brought to Susan and her husband, Gary:

Harley, aged eleven, died at 6:50 a.m. on Sunday, October 3, 2010, the day when many Episcopal and Catholic churches observe the Feast of Saint Francis and hold special services to bless animals. . . . One of his most endearing traits earned him the moniker "Rescue Kitty." If one of the other cats was trapped in a closet or in the garage, Harley would find Susan or Gary and meow while pawing at their legs, prompting the human response, "What's wrong, Lassie? Is Timmy trapped under the tractor again?" He would then lead Susan or Gary to the appropriate door and paw at it until they opened it to free the other cat. . . . When Susan and Gary's cat Belphoebe had to be euthanized several years ago, Harley's role as "Rescue Kitty" became especially poignant. He traveled in circles around the house, examining each door he found, as if hoping that Phoebe would be behind it. Susan finally told him, "Harley, she's behind a door we can't open." . . . Rest in peace, Harley. You're behind a door we can't open, but you're finally Outside, where you always wanted to go. We hope you're having splendid adventures.[5]

Susan published this obituary—and many others for her feline friends—in her blog. Given the lukewarm reception to pet obits in traditional media, many pet keepers have gravitated to the internet and social media to publicly share their heartfelt tributes for their beloved animals. Dozens of websites are now available for people to post pet memorials and purchase pet-loss memorabilia. In a study of how Americans memorialize their pets, the most popular option was through posting about the pet on social media.[6] Two-thirds of the study participants posted about their pet's death online, though only about 20 percent created a formal obituary. Though most people do not craft an obituary for their pet, studies have shown that doing so can be beneficial because writing about their pet helps people process their loss.[7] Although I would argue that sharing our pet stories with the people who know us best—and who know our animals—is far more beneficial and healing than posting a picture and a few words online, any outlet for our grief is better than none.

## Laying Our Pets to Rest

Starting in the late seventeenth century, people's desire to honor their animal companions in traditional ways led to the creation of pet cemeteries in Europe and the US. Though not officially sanctioned by mainline religious institutions as sacred ground, pet cemeteries are sacred to animal lovers everywhere.

One of the most famous pet cemeteries is also one of the oldest, at least in the US. The Hartsdale Pet Cemetery was founded in 1896 in what was then a rural area just north of New York City. Incorporated in 1914, Hartsdale is now home to more than 70,000 deceased animals, primarily cats and dogs but also birds, rabbits, the occasional monkey or snake, and even a lion interred in 1908 by a Hungarian princess. The emergence of pet cemeteries like Hartsdale can be linked to changing public sentiments about animals. As incomes rose and the middle class emerged in the late 1800s and early 1900s, keeping animals as companions also grew. Convinced that their animals have souls just as people do and deserve to be buried in sacred ground, activists rallied for the right to be buried with their pets. Despite their passionate appeals to church leaders, however, these activists were unable to convince religious institutions that animals had the same right to burial on consecrated ground as people. To this day, interring animals in human cemeteries, especially those on church or temple grounds, is illegal in most American states.

The growth of the pet funerary business is a contemporary example of the same social phenomenon that fueled the establishment of pet cemeteries a century ago. In response to a burgeoning market for formal pet funerals, pet funerary businesses have become one of the fastest-growing segments of the funerary industry. These businesses offer all the services associated with traditional funeral homes, including memorial services, private pet cremation, wake ceremonies, individual pet burial on cemetery grounds, headstones, bone vaults, cremation urns, and memorabilia. Services are expensive, so only a relatively small portion of pet keepers can afford them. Yet the fact that they exist at all is evidence of people's desire to honor their pets in traditional ways.

Pet cemeteries offer particularly interesting insights into the hearts and minds of the pet-keeping public. A study by anthropologist Stanley Brandes chronicles the pet gravestones located in Hartsdale.[8] Gravestones represent the final words that will forever be tied to a beloved animal, and many pet keepers take great care in choosing inscriptions. Brandes discovered that inscriptions became more overtly religious in tone starting in the early 1990s, and many gravestones also began incorporating the cross, the Star of David, and other religious symbols. According to Brandes, these "gravestone inscriptions and designs . . . bestow a religious identity upon deceased pets. They express the owner's belief in an afterlife for the pets, as well as the expectation, or at least the hope, that owners and pets will be reunited in the afterlife. . . . The deceased often have first names and surnames, kinship affiliations, religious and ethnic identity, immortal souls, and even personal and emotional features that parallel those of human children."[9] Pet keepers regularly visit the graves of their beloved pets at Hartsdale, often on holidays and to mark important anniversaries. Many leave toys or other pet possessions on the graves. It's customary for visitors to leave small rocks or pebbles on top of pet gravestones, a practice borrowed from the Jewish tradition for human loved ones.

In the book *Good Grief: On Loving Pets, Here and Hereafter*, pet enthusiast E. B. Bartels writes about visiting Hartsdale and looking at the grave stones. There was one stone in particular that caught her eye: "CLARENCE, it read. MY ETERNAL FRIEND AND GUARDIAN ANGEL. YOU'LL ALWAYS BE A PART OF ME FOREVER. And underneath, obscured by flowers: LOVE, M."[10] Later, Bartels realized she was looking at the grave of Mariah Carey's cat. "I had read about Clarence," Bartels writes. "I knew he was a loyal friend, kind, affectionate, sweet. Even though he ran with a famous crowd, he didn't seem to care about money or celebrity or power. He valued the simple things in life. . . . [He] was eighteen when he died—by most cemeteries' standards, painfully young. But in this cemetery, in Hartsdale, New York, eighteen is a good, long life."[11]

## Honoring Animal Lives

In the majestic red rock canyons outside the small town of Kanab in southern Utah, a remarkable animal sanctuary offers a place of healing for animals and the people who love them. According to its website (bestfriends.org), the Best Friends Animal Sanctuary "is the healing home for up to 1,600 dogs, cats, birds, bunnies, horses, pigs and other animals. . . . The largest sanctuary of its kind in the U.S., Best Friends has become the heart of a collaborative no-kill movement, and a model for the future of animal welfare."[12]

Every month, the Utah sanctuary holds a memorial service for animals who have died in the sanctuary as well as the pets of sanctuary staff and volunteers and people who contribute to the organization. The services are recorded and posted online so that people from all over the world can participate virtually. The setting for these ceremonies is called "Angels Rest," and it's a breathtaking place, with benches arranged in front of a small pavilion that overlooks a memorial garden filled with stones and wind chimes commemorating animals who've passed.

The half-hour memorial services typically begin with a non-denominational sermon in which speakers share reflections about animals, people, altruism, empathy, life, death, and many other topics. Next, the names of the animals who've passed in the sanctuary are read, one by one, as their pictures flash on the screen. Then, it's story time. Pet keepers from all over the world send in stories about their deceased pets. The stories are read out loud while pet photos are displayed onscreen. Many of the stories reference pets crossing over the rainbow bridge and emphasize the pet keeper's belief that they will one day be reunited with their pet. The sentiments expressed in these heartfelt tribute mirrors what I've heard from many pet keepers: how their animals were special, intuitive, and empathetic; how they brought joy and laughter to their days; how they taught them life lessons about love, courage, resilience, and the importance of play; and, of course, how much people miss their animal friends when they lose them.

The monthly services offered at the Best Friends Animal Sanctuary are beautiful and inspiring. Unfortunately, such services are also relatively rare in the US. Most people hold ceremonies for their pets in private rather than in public. The traditional rituals that originated in religious practice often guide informal death ceremonies for pets, even for people who are not particularly religious. An Australian study of pet loss and religion found that almost half of respondents held a ceremony for their pets and most followed traditional funeral norms, including eulogies, wakes, and prayers.[13] Many also placed crosses or other religious symbols on their pets' graves. Holding a ceremony was as common among people who did not identify as religious as among those who did

Although we don't have many opportunities to honor the passing of our beloved animals in public, I'm confident that where there is a will, there is a way. As a pet chaplain, I've attended and sometimes presided over wonderful celebrations of a pet's life in which people look at photos, sing songs, say prayers, and share their memories. People laugh as tears run down their faces while recalling funny and touching events in a pet's life. It's wonderful to see people pull together to share their joy and sorrow, and it is through such fellowship that we can truly heal form our losses.

When we observe our losses with ceremonies—even very simple ones—we demonstrate that the lives of our animals matter. By publicly acknowledging the tremendous gifts we receive from our animal companions and the lessons we can learn from their example, we challenge the widespread belief that animals are lesser creatures than people and their deaths a trivial matter. Every prayer and every ceremony is another square in a metaphorical quilt of remembrance. By bringing animals into the fold of our spirituality, we can offer a new vision of our connection with animals and, indeed, with all life on this planet.

# Animal Ambassadors

Our pets transform our lives. This is one of the lessons that my friend Mary DeRosa learned after losing her cat Linus. I met Mary, a writer and filmmaker, when she participated in my veterinary chaplaincy course. Like many of the people who took the course, Mary was a lifelong animal lover who was passionate about animal rescue. "Animals are all day, every day for me," Mary told me when we spoke. "My rescue work is really my calling. I just have to work with and for animals."

Mary began her rescue work in 2015 at a no-kill shelter after Linus died suddenly. "Linus was this amazing cat," Mary said. "My then husband and I called him the 'ambassador of goodwill.' We'd had him since he was a tiny kitten, and he loved everyone. He knew no strangers. Fabulous cat. But then one night we walked in the house, saw Linus on the couch, and all of a sudden, he just seized up and fell off the couch. We rushed over and scooped him up, but he was gone. We took him to the emergency vet, but it was too late. We found out later that he'd had a heart attack."

Mary was devastated. She said it's hard to lose any animal you love, and she's had to euthanize many of her pets. But watching Linus die before her eyes was a big shock. "I remember feeling that I needed to do something to deal with my grief," Mary said. "I don't know why I thought about animal rescue, but I guess I thought that helping other people or helping the animals would help me feel better. And it did. My rescue work helped me get out of my head. I also think it was just God saying, 'It's time. You're going to do this.' So my love for Linus and my grief for him booted me into my rescue work, and once I was into it, I didn't ever want to get out of it. It's sad sometimes, and I get angry. But it's totally worth it. I can't imagine not doing this work."

Today, Mary volunteers at the pet rescue every Saturday morning, and on Sunday mornings, she volunteers at a rescue dedicated to pigs and other farm animals. Her interest in helping animals traditionally viewed as food occurred gradually, over many years. For Mary, her faith played a big role. I mentioned in chapter 8 that Mary feels morally obligated to be a good steward for God's creation. At some point in her life, she realized she could no longer participate with a clear conscience in an industrial food system that treats animals as unfeeling objects. She no longer eats animals, and although many people don't entirely understand her choice, those who know her are very respectful of her decision. At the non-denominational Christian church she attends, her fellow congregants regularly ask her how the pigs at the sanctuary are doing.

Mary said she loves both rescues where she volunteers, but the pig rescue holds a special place in her heart because so few people realize that pigs are smart and very emotional—a lot like the dogs and cats she cares for at the pet rescue. "I've met people who say things like, 'You mean you only have pigs at this rescue? Just pigs? Why do pigs need rescuing?'" Mary said. "But I've discovered that the pigs are really amazing. There are a hundred and eighty pigs at the rescue, and I've noticed they form cliques and bonds and communities. They scold each other and love on each other and disagree with each other. They're just like dogs or small children. They feel the same things we do, and they behave in similar ways. They remember you. They know the crazy lady in the MINI Cooper always brings baby carrots and Oreos when she shows up. When they see my car, their heads pop up, and as soon as I park, they're right there at the door. They're just amazing, and I wish everybody could somehow grasp that they're not just this commodity. They're living beings."

Mary struggles to understand why so many people draw a hard line between their dogs and cats and other animals who aren't that different from their pets. This dissonance is common among people in the animal advocacy movement, but Mary has encountered the same sort of dissonance in the pet-keeping world. She told me a story about a woman who took in her son's cat because her daughter-in-law was pregnant and worried that the cat would sit on the baby's face and suffocate it. But the woman soon tired of caring for the cat, so she took her to a veterinarian and asked that the cat be euthanized. The veterinarian refused because the cat was healthy.

"This woman was just genuinely befuddled as to why that was a problem," Mary said. "And she was the sweetest lady in the world. So even people who are normal, caring individuals will do things like that, and to me it's just so bizarre. It's a weird experience when you meet people who are wonderful human beings, and yet they're somehow oblivious to animals. I think it's just social conditioning because we're taught to believe that animals are just animals, and they're just here for our entertainment or for us to eat or for us to fumigate or get rid of or look at. The same thing happens when you lose a pet. I don't understand how people cannot have empathy for someone who loses a pet and how they can't see the loss of an animal as something monumental. But some people just don't see that."

I suspect almost every person who devotes time and energy to helping animals and advocating for their interests has a Linus somewhere in their past. All the people I met in my veterinary chaplaincy course shared stories about pets who had changed their lives, including many, like Mary, who were compelled to get involved in animal rescue and advocacy after losing a cherished pet. When we enjoy a loving, mutually beneficial relationship with an animal, it becomes very difficult to think of that animal as an object we can use without considering their feelings and needs.

As we've seen, we tend to draw hard lines between the animals we keep as pets and those who fall outside our circle of love and care. Yet our animal friends can sometimes change this perspective. For people like Mary, the lives of all animals matter, and she feels morally obligated to do everything she can to protect them. When we make this transition, we can begin to appreciate how deeply we're all connected.

## Animals as Change Agents

The surge in pet keeping in the developed West began in the 1980s and accelerated at the turn of the century. Since 2000, the growth in the US pet industry—measured in terms of the number of households that keep pets, money spent on pets, and employment in pet services—is astounding. Here's a slice of the story by the numbers:

- Pet keeping in the US has more than tripled since the 1970s. As of 2025, 71 percent of US households kept a pet, totaling 94 million households.[1]
- An estimated 45 percent of US households keep dogs, and the population of pet dogs increased 16 percent between 2016 and 2020.[2]
- An estimated 26 percent of US households keep cats, and the population of pet cats increased 7 percent between 2016 and 2020.[3]

Pet keeping in the US is nothing short of a massive cultural phenomenon. As we've welcomed animals into our homes, the proportion of people who regard their pets as full-fledged family members has also increased. According to the AVMA, nearly all pet keepers (95 percent) consider their pets to be members of their families—up four percentage points from 2012 and seven points since the question was first asked in 2007.[4]

How is this pet-keeping tsunami impacting the dominant Western attitudes about animals? Is anthropocentrism declining in the face of this rolling tide of pet love, like a sandbar giving way under the force of powerful waves? I believe it is. Our animals are change agents. When you fall in love with an animal, you inevitably begin to think about them very differently than you did before the experience.

I'm reminded of a story a young man named Bryan shared with me after losing his dog, Ringo. Bryan told me that his wife, Gwen, had never been around animals, and the idea of an animal in the house was foreign to her. She didn't dislike animals, but she didn't understand why someone would allow an animal into their home, much less become emotionally attached to them. "In many ways, a dog was no different than a wild bird to Gwen," Bryan said. "She had no real emotional connection to dogs. But she knew I liked animals and that we would eventually get a dog. There was no way around it."

After fostering some dogs through their local rescue, the couple eventually adopted Ringo, a cantankerous terrier who'd been adopted three times and returned to the shelter three times because of his temperament. It took a few years, but Ringo eventually became very affectionate and protective of his human family, and he was particularly close to Gwen. The two were inseparable, and Ringo would do things for Gwen that he refused to do for Bryan. Bryan was surprised and pleased by the change. "I think Gwen began to realize how much these animals liked us," he said. "She began to see animals differently. There's something to be said for having a person, child, or animal who doesn't like anyone else except you. It makes you feel special. And Ringo was very attached to Gwen."

When Ringo was about fifteen years old, his health began to decline, and Bryan knew from his experience as a vet tech that he wouldn't survive long. He and Gwen had done everything they could to ready themselves for the day they would have to say goodbye, but nothing prepared the couple for the emotional gut punch they felt when Ringo died. That's when they decided to come to my pet loss support group.

"I seriously could not function when Ringo died," Bryan said. "I just couldn't seem to snap out of my funk. I cried a lot, which is unusual for me. But the thing that shocked me the most when we came to the support group—and that still shocks me—was when Gwen said that when Ringo passed away, it was harder for her than when her mom passed away. Knowing what I know of her, that she had no interest in animals and that she didn't even want a dog, I was shocked to hear her say that. But now I realize that Ringo was her baby. He was really the first animal that she connected with. He helped her see what I had always seen in animals and why I like animals. He bonded us together. He was really our first child."

It's certainly remarkable that someone with no experience with animals might fall in love with a pet and realize that animals are wonderful companions. But a special animal like Ringo can also change the perspective of someone who has spent their entire life around animals. One of the vet tech students I interviewed, a young woman named Lillian, grew up on a farm surrounded by all kinds of animals. She'd kept many pets throughout her life, but it wasn't until she met her cat Freddie that she really understood the true power of the human-animal bond. "If you've never had that bond, you don't really understand when people refer to their dog as their baby or have cute, affectionate nicknames for their pets," Lillian said. "Or you have a little less patience for somebody who puts their cat in a baby carriage. It's a little too much. OK, I admit it, the cat probably doesn't like it. But once you understand the bond, you have more patience with people who do things like that. People go crazy for their pets, and it's a big deal for them. The human-animal bond is a big deal, and you have to respect it."

Like Lillian, countless pet keepers have learned that pets have much to teach us about living in right relationship with each other and other living creatures. As pet keeping continues to grow in popularity, it's possible that our pets can also have a positive impact on the way we view all animals and the natural world.

## Liminal Creatures

Animals have always been a part of our lives. In ancient times, we lived as brethren, sometimes foes and sometimes friends, but always in close, daily contact with each other. We hunted animals and were hunted by them. We studied their behavior and often emulated their hunting tactics, pitting spears, arrows, and our cunning minds against tooth and claw. We were inspired by their beautiful coats of fur, colorful plumes, and shimmering scales, and we mimicked their beauty in our dress and their movements in our dance. In northern climates, we often lived in close quarters with the domesticated animals we depended on for our survival, sharing a single dwelling to survive harsh winters.

Today, we inhabit this earth alongside other animals just as our ancestors did, but the way we live in relationship with our fellow creatures is radically different. In the modern West, an increasing number of people live in vast, densely populated urban areas. Most animals have been relegated to cages, small islands of land between roadways and housing developments, remote patches of sparsely peopled lands, and, increasingly, to a virtual world. We're more likely to interact with animals indirectly or symbolically than physically. We see representations of animals in videos, photographs, and digital images rendered with startling detail on our screens. Children's books, TV shows, and movies are filled with friendly animals who often bear only a slight resemblance to the creatures who inspired these creative interpretations. Sports teams are often named after fierce, charismatic species like bears, panthers, and lions. Yet what happens on those synthetic playing fields has little to do with the actual beings who live in the wild, struggling to survive in shrinking patches of wilderness.

When it comes to living, breathing animals, we most often encounter the wild variety on occasional excursions to a zoo or an aquarium.

Depending on where we live, we rarely come across a wolf, bear, or other wild animal in person—an experience that is at once frightening and thrilling. We're less thrilled by animals such as rabbits, squirrels, deer, and coyotes who get too close to our homes and are considered lawn-and-garden nuisances. For me, encountering animals virtually and simultaneously losing contact with living animals is an alarming trend. I worry that someday we'll only experience the wonder of a hummingbird or the magnificence of an elephant as an assemblage of pixels on a high-resolution screen.

Our animal companions are an important exception to this trend. Pets occupy a unique position in the human-built world and the larger, natural world. Our dogs, cats, hamsters, birds, horses, and other pets are liminal creatures who serve as a bridge between our cities and suburbs and the vast, mysterious world of the untamed wilderness. Unlike animals who live their daily lives independently and remain a mystery to most of us, our pets share our most intimate spaces. We know and understand them in ways that we're unable to know and understand the wild animals in our midst.

In fact, for many pet keepers, their companion animal may be their *only* connection to the natural world and its many healthful benefits. Scientists have established that contact with natural landscapes, even the simple act of sitting under a tree, can lower your blood pressure and reduce stress in much the same way that animals do.[5] Is it any wonder that, as rapid urban development and environmental destruction impinge on our access to natural areas, we bring nature into our homes through the beautiful faces, bodies, and loving energy of our pets?

This idea is more than mere supposition. Studies have shown that people with an affinity for nature also tend to like animals and keep pets, and that, in turn, pet keeping encourages concern for wild animals and the environment. Known as the *pets as ambassadors hypothesis*, this theory was developed by animal ethicists James Serpell and Elizabeth Paul in 1994.[6] The theory holds that contact with pets can promote positive attitudes toward all animals and serve as a springboard toward concerns for other kinds of animals and nature. As noted by the authors of a Canadian study of the ambassadors hypothesis, "Childhood pet keeping was found to be (retrospectively) associated with more positive attitudes toward animals (in general) later in life. People who had pets during their childhood were also more likely to report participating in organizations that advocate in favor of animal welfare, to avoid meat products out of ethical or moral reasons (i.e., vegetarianism, veganism, etc.), and to endorse more positive attitudes toward farm, wild, and laboratory animals."[7]

Though intriguing, the pets as ambassadors theory is not without its complexities. Pet keeping is generally not considered a form of animal advocacy, and it is arguable whether our modern pet craze improves or degrades the well-being of dogs, cats, and other species commonly kept as pets. Some people in the animal rights movement object to pet keeping as an unethical, exploitative, and harmful practice. I understand this sentiment, though I don't share it. Although many animals suffer because of the excesses of the pet industry, keeping pets brings many benefits to our lives and the lives of the animals we love.

My work with pet keepers supports the validity of the pets as ambassadors hypothesis. I've met many people like Gwen and Lillian whose perspective about animals shifted dramatically after they experienced a loving relationship with a pet. And I'm constantly reminded of the power of animals to change our hearts and minds, and I firmly believe that pet keeping can push our habitual anthropocentric worldview in a more animal-friendly direction. As I've said, an increasing number of people are expressing their love for animals by advocating for them. Some, like Mary DeRosa, get involved in animal rescue after losing a pet as a way of honoring their pet's legacy. Others have chosen a plant-based diet after visiting an animal sanctuary, looking into a cow's big brown eyes, and realizing that the experience was a lot like looking into the eyes of their beloved dog. I'm hopeful that as pet keeping continues to grow in the West and around the world, the number of people willing to broaden their circle of love beyond their pets will rise as well.

There's another important way our animal companions serve as ambassadors, and it lies in the way they bring joy, happiness, and a sense of meaningful connection to others into our lives. My friend Kim McCool shared the story of a woman in a hospital who was completely withdrawn from the world, as if she were waiting to die. She refused to eat and wouldn't respond to anyone—not the hospital staff or her family and friends. When Kim brought her therapy dog Frankie to the woman's room, she asked the woman if it would be OK if Frankie got up on the bed with her. The woman nodded, which was the first time in weeks she had responded to a person. When Frankie curled up next to her, the woman began to stroke his head. Before long, she began to talk about her own dogs, who she said loved to eat. Kim told her that Frankie also loved food and would eat just about anything except blueberries. The woman smiled and said the same was true of her dogs. This exchange eventually led to a broader pastoral conversation about many other aspects of her life.

What happened in that hospital room is what I call the "pet portal." Pets have a way of opening a line directly to our hearts, and when we enter this portal, we may be privileged to enter someone's inner world and bear witness to their joys and sorrows. This is the essence of spiritual care, and animals are the key. They are, in fact, "ambassadors of happy," which is how Kim refers to Frankie.

## CHAPTER 12

# Animal Dreams

I sometimes dream about animals, but there's one dream that I've never forgotten. I was standing before a large group of animals: dogs, cats, birds, cows, pigs, horses, buffalo, giraffes, elephants, and so on. They were all staring at me, and their ghostly expressions reminded me of the haunting figure in Edvard Munch's painting *The Scream*. Their mouths and eyes were wide and dark, like empty black holes, as if they were lifeless shells with furred, feathered, and finned outsides but no insides. The animals were crying out for me to help them because humans had stolen their souls. I remember feeling terrified and helpless to relieve their suffering. I desperately sought help from my friends, visited a judge and a minister, and tried to get the media's attention. But no one would listen.

For me, this troubling dream highlights the fact that animals have no voice to defend themselves—at least not voices we can easily hear. Animals communicate with us in all kinds of ways, and in ancient times, many people knew how to listen. But people today speak so loudly—and there are so many human voices shouting all the time—that we fail to hear the voices of the animals. One of the goals of this book and the other books in the Pet Chaplain Learning Series is to elevate the voices of our animal companions by acknowledging and celebrating the profound ways they enrich our lives and envision ways we can enrich theirs. When we share our pet stories with others, we speak on our animals' behalf, and I believe this is a profoundly important task if we're to reshape the false narrative about animals we've inherited from our forebears.

Complex challenges lie ahead. How do we offer the best care possible to the animals we love and simultaneously meet our need for love and companionship? How can we bring pets into our spiritual lives without compromising the dignity of people who don't see animals as we do? Thinking beyond our personal concerns, how do we balance the needs of a rapidly growing human population with those of other life-forms? How do we repair the damage that has been wrought on this earth because of centuries of anthropocentric thinking and behavior? And what new values can we embrace that might eventually lead to a sustainable future?

I don't have ready answers to these questions, and I wouldn't presume to have them. Big questions like these are best explored collectively, and it will most likely be a very long time before we fully understand how we've answered them. Perhaps this book has helped with this task. I hope you've felt inspired to reflect on your personal beliefs about animals and where those beliefs come from. Better yet, I hope you've had the opportunity to share this journey with others. And maybe you've also begun to think about the world we've inherited as well as the world you want to create.

For my coauthor Karen Duke and me, creating this book and the other books in the Pet Chaplain Learning Series has been an incredible journey of learning and self-discovery. We've discovered a lot about animals—including the human animal—and about ourselves. In this final chapter, I'll share my reflections on some of the topics explored in this book. As we've seen, our animal companions change our lives for the better. We love them dearly, and it's a rare kind of love—innocent, unpretentious, uncomplicated, steadfast. And because we love our pets, we're willing to change the world for them. But this is not an easy task. Ideological barriers, legal hurdles, corporate profit-seeking, social conflict, and institutional and cultural inertia stand in the way of a more respectful, balanced relationship with our animal brethren. It's hard to know where to begin when the challenges we're facing are so vast. Yet I believe in starting small with whatever is most within our control. Ultimately, the only thing any of us has much control over is the choices we make in our daily lives. From there, however, extraordinary things can happen.

## Telling a New Story About Animals

We've long patronized animals because we've been taught that they're lesser creatures than human beings. We denigrate and oppress them because of our deep-seated anxiety about death—a tendency most of us are not even aware of. Some people assert that God loves us more than the rest of creation, as if we're the only part of creation that matters. We also tend to see the world through a mechanistic, empirical lens, one that casts our fellow creatures and the natural world into rigid hierarchical systems that, in their simplicity, distort reality. Because of these misconceptions, we've cut ourselves off from nature and struggle to find authentic connections with other living beings.

It's easy to cast stones at the anthropocentric worldview we've inherited. Yet we're all creatures of our culture, and we're all caught in the web of our society's dominant narrative about the world. This has always been true for human beings. Plato and Aristotle based their understandings of the cosmos on the pagan beliefs they'd inherited from their ancestors and combined them with new understandings of the human capacity for reason. Early Christian theologians worked within the hierarchical view of the cosmos they'd inherited from the Greeks, refining those ideas to fit with emerging Christian doctrine. Descartes and other scientists who participated in Western Europe's Scientific Revolution adapted these ideas further to accommodate new understandings of the physical world. Every individual takes what they know and believe about the world and integrates it with new understandings through a constant process of learning and reframing.

People today are no different. The way we view the world is a story we've inherited and modified to make sense of the universe and our place in it. As I've said, ideas can be tenacious, especially when they serve our immediate interests. The point is that the anthropocentric worldview that has long dominated the West is not an absolute truth. It's a social construct born of a particular place and time and shaped by a complex array of philosophical, scientific, economic, religious, psychological, and social forces. It's a story we've inherited and that many people continue to believe. We're currently living in the *Anthropocene*, the age of humans, and our ingrained habit of thinking of animals as lesser beings plays out in countless ways. As we've seen, some of these practices seem relatively benign while others are harmful to people, animals, and the planet.

But cultures *do* change, and paradigms *do* shift, although slowly and often painfully. The age-old story about animals that has long dominated our world is beginning to change, and the social and religious disenfranchisement that pet keepers experience today is evidence of our society's growing pains. Shedding old ways of seeing and embracing a new and more accurate perspective of the greater-than-human world is good and necessary. But such a profound transformation is also challenging and entails a kind of grief.

Individually and collectively, we're grieving what has been lost—the promise of a utopian society grounded in reason, technology, science, and the control of nature. Simultaneously, we're grieving the less-than-utopian result of that vision. And where there is grief, there is also despair. In *The More Beautiful World Our Hearts Know Is Possible*, philosopher Charles Eisenstein explores the paradigm shift underway in the way we think about animals and nature. "Despair is part of the territory we must traverse. . . ," writes Eisenstein. "True optimism comes from having traversed the territory of despair and taken its measure. It is not ignorant of the magnitude of the crisis nor unaware of the forces that stand in the path of healing."[1]

By necessity, the new story we tell about people, animals, and our place in the natural world will differ from the one that ancient peoples told simply because our lives are so different. When the foundational ideas we've reviewed in this book were taking shape, the world was far more agrarian and much less populous than it is now. That world didn't include the internet, global shipping, or large-scale industry and agriculture. It also didn't include puppy mills; shelters that euthanize unwanted animals by the hundreds every day; the factory farming of cows, pigs, and chickens; commercial fishing; or laboratory testing of animals. In many ways, our modern world seems completely irrational if not completely insane. It certainly falls far short of the perfectly rational utopia that Plato envisioned.

Perhaps the change we need to make in our lives should begin with a simple paradigm shift: we must accept that we're animals. This statement may appear to be tongue in cheek. You might be thinking, "Of course we're animals." After all, Darwin and other scientists who followed in his footsteps have offered us ample proof of this fact. But do we really, truly, *deeply* own our animal-ness? How comfortable are we with our own animal natures and our animal bodies?

## Being Animal

In the discussion of Ernest Becker's work in chapter 3, we learned that we humans habitually separate ourselves from other animals, and this impulse can be attributed to our unconscious anxiety about death. This impulse is evident in Christian teachings that exalt the soul and the heavenly realm and simultaneously denigrate the body and the earthly, physical realm. Animals, who are believed to have no immortal souls, are denigrated not only for their lack of reason but because of their *animal-ness*. They're often portrayed in unflattering ways that don't reflect the reality of their lives. Yes, they defecate and mate openly, and wild animals fight tooth and claw for survival. But many also live peaceably with each other and cooperate to achieve their goals.

Our habit of denigrating the body and the physical realm of existence is one of the reasons we work so hard to deny the fact that we, too, are animals. We seek immortality with the same fervor that compelled our ancestors to travel the world in search of the fountain of youth. In the twenty-first century, scientists are toying with human and animal genomes and dabbling with the possibility that, through technology, we can become less animal, less susceptible to disease and aging, more intelligent, and, ultimately, immortal. Taken to extremes, some people seem to want to become more machine than animal. Transhumanism represents humankind's latest attempt to distance ourselves from our imperfect, animal bodies. In the opening lines of the book *How to Be Animal*, author Melanie Challenger succinctly captures the paradox that characterizes the transhumanist movement: "The world is now dominated by an animal that doesn't think it's an animal. And the future is being imagined by an animal that doesn't want to be an animal."[2]

There's no doubt that we're one of the most powerful creatures on the planet. We're extraordinarily creative, and our ability to imagine and make what we imagine real sets us apart from many of our fellow creatures. The question then becomes a matter of what we're doing with our creative abilities. What kind of world have we created? If we look at all we've accomplished in the last two millennia, can anyone truly judge it to be good, as God judged his original creation to be good?

It's folly to believe we can flourish separately from nature or to think that the laws of nature—and even the immutable law of death itself—don't apply to us. The survival of all life on this planet, including our own species, is in peril because of our vaunted accomplishments. Technologically, we've tipped the laws of nature exclusively to the advantage of our short-term interests. In doing so, we've created an astonishing imbalance in the natural world. Today, there are far more domesticated animals than there are wild animals on this planet. If you were to weigh every mammal on earth, livestock makes up about two-thirds of the total biomass, humans account for about a third, and wild animals make up only 4 percent.[3] What a strange and remarkably unbalanced world we've created in the name of human progress.

Perhaps we humans are far too clever for our own good—or, more accurately, perhaps we're more clever than wise. We celebrate our gift for reason and rationality, yet we often use this faculty to rationalize our behavior and ignore anything that doesn't serve our desires. We have many gifts, and we've created many wondrous things, from beautiful works of art and music to powerful technological inventions. Yet we often lack the imagination to foresee the long-term effects of what we're creating in real time. We also suffer from hubris. From a Christian theological perspective, the anthropocentrism that characterizes Western culture shows that we have committed the original sin of false pride. We insist that human beings are closer to God than the rest of creation, and we denigrate other living creatures as lesser beings—less intelligent, less complex emotionally, less everything. In doing so, far too many of us have lost touch with our innate connection to the natural world and fail to appreciate the simple gifts and life lessons offered by the animals in our midst.

As we've seen, however, social currents that challenge this mindset are gaining strength as more people question the assumptions we've long held about ourselves and other animals. Our love affair with pets is one of those currents. Our deep sense of connection with our animal friends reflects our collective need to reclaim our connection with nature at a time when it is most threatened. As noted by Marc Bekoff, "We need animals in our lives just as we need air to breathe. . . . Without close and reciprocal relationships with other animal beings, we're alienated from the rich, diverse, and magnificent world in which we live."[4] Our pets connect us with the natural world and satisfy our longing for reliable companionship, nonjudgmental love, soothing physical contact, and authentic emotional connection in an age when our communities are increasingly divided, families are split up, and divorce rates are high. Many people struggle to maintain fulfilling relationships with their fellow human beings, and for these souls, pets can be a lifeline.

Our pets change us, often for the better. They teach us a great deal about living in right relationship with other species and the natural world. They help us understand and embrace the beauty of our animal natures and bring our bodies, minds, hearts, and souls to our relationships. They also help us learn to love each other more and judge less; to forgive more readily and lay down the burden of past hurts; to offer ourselves authentically to each other, just as we are; to bring the comfort of our presence to those who are suffering; to be loyal companions whom others can trust; to share the warmth of our touch; to embrace each moment with joy; and to share the pleasure of simple, unhurried play. Being an animal, it turns out, is a pretty good thing.

## I-Thou

After giving some thought to the animal you are and your feelings about this topic, I encourage you to widen your focus and consider the animals in your life. What can you do to embrace them in all their wonderful, messy animal-ness?

In chapter 1, we took a critical look at the human-animal bond, which is defined as a mutually beneficial relationship between people and animals. Practicing true reciprocity in a relationship with an animal requires recognizing their needs as an individual and honoring the inherent value of their life. This is not easily accomplished. I fear that at times love can blind us to the actual needs of our animal companions, and it's easy to overlook the fact that they're not furry people. They're unique creatures with unique perceptual realities that differ from ours. Because animals can't tell us in words how they feel or what they want, we may have unrealistic expectations for them or inadvertently put them into situations that make them feel uncomfortable or fearful.

A helpful ethical framework we can turn to for guidance draws on the work of German existential philosopher Martin Buber. In 1923 Buber introduced the critical distinction between what he called "I-thou" and "I-it" relationships with the publication of *Ich und Du* (I and Thou).[5] Buber believed that each person (and I would add each animal) participates in the divine. When we treat other people or animals as *thou*, we honor them as spiritual beings. Conversely, when we treat other people or animals as mere objects—an *it*—we deny their sacred nature, and our interactions become purely transactional and lack depth and meaning.

Buber believed that all living beings participate in the divine and are worthy of being addressed as *thou*. A rabbi friend of mine shared a personal story about Buber that speaks to this perspective. Late in his life, Buber was a guest lecturer at a rabbinic college in the Midwestern US. My friend was a student at the time. He recalled that it was a beautiful day when Buber arrived in the classroom for his lecture, and Buber invited the class to meet beneath the spreading branches of a large tree in the school commons. The students sat in the shade, waiting for Buber to begin his lecture, but he remained silent. One student nervously asked him when he would begin his lecture. Buber replied that he had already begun. The students were perplexed, and that's when Buber asked them to consider their relationship with the tree. My friend, who eventually became a rabbi in the Reform movement, marveled at Buber's insight, and that experience remained one of the most meaningful of his religious education.

So what constitutes being treated as a respected *thou* versus an *it*? The celebrated psychologist Abraham H. Maslow offers some insight into this query. A student of human behavior, Maslow penned a scholarly article titled "A Theory of Human Motivation" in 1943 in which he identified five levels of human needs and wants. He arranged these levels in a hierarchical pyramid.[6] Our basic physiological needs of food, water, and shelter form the base of the pyramid, followed in ascending order by safety and security, love and belonging, and self-esteem. At the peak of this metaphorical pyramid lies what Maslow called "self-actualization," which is defined as "realizing personal potential, self-fulfillment, seeking personal growth, and peak experiences."[7] Self-actualization is an ideal because many barriers stand in the way of personal fulfillment, including poverty, illness, and social alienation. In fact, Maslow believed that self-actualization is exceedingly rare, though he claimed that we periodically experience moments of self-actualization, which he called "peak" experiences.

I bring up this well-known psychological model of human needs and motivation because it provides a helpful way to frame how non-human animals might seek to lead rich, fulfilling lives. To return to Buber's conception of the I-thou sacred relationship, interacting with an animal in a way that honors them as a *thou* requires striving to understand their unique sensory experience of the world and honoring that experience as much as possible. This requires a basic understanding of the way different species engage with the world and a good imagination, or what psychologist and dog olfaction expert Alexandra Horowitz refers to as "an informed imaginative leap."[8] Consider the sensory experience of a dog. With their keen sense of smell, dogs experience the world in a profoundly different way than we do because we're strongly oriented toward sight. According to Horowitz, dogs live in a "state of olfactory exploration all the time."[9] She believes we must "let dogs be dogs," so she regularly takes Finn, her affable black lab, on sniffing walks and allows him to engage as long as he would like with the many tantalizing smells he encounters.[10]

In recent decades, pet keepers have begun to realize the benefits—both to themselves and particularly to their animals—of honoring their animals as a respected *thou*. This requires paying attention to much more than an animal's basic need for food, water, and shelter. These conscientious pet keepers study animal behavior and physiology to better understand the traits that are common to their pet's species as well as their animal's unique quirks and style of communication. They provide the best food and medical care their pocketbook allows as well as suitable exercise, mental stimulation, and social opportunities for their pets. In these ways and more, they strive to honor the mutually beneficial spirit of the human-animal bond. The result is happier, healthier animals.

One of the vet tech students I interviewed, a man named Frank, had a lot to say about the balance that's necessary if we're to truly enjoy a mutually beneficial relationship with an animal. Frank had grown up on the farm, where he learned to interact with animals as useful objects. But his cat Muppet, who he adopted as an adult, changed his perspective. "When I was growing up and taking care of animals, I had to feed them and water them, but I didn't appreciate the quality of their life at the time," he said. "Well, there's a difference between giving basic care and giving quality of life. You can care for a human or an animal and give them the basic necessities. Or you can take that same person or animal and give them understanding and love and a good quality of life, and I think you get all of that back."

Frank's comments highlight the importance of reciprocity in our relationships with our animal friends. In the wonderful book *Braiding Sweetgrass*, author Robin Wall Kimmerer, a botanist and member of Oklahoma's Citizen Potawatomi Nation, explores the concept of reciprocity and its vital role in Indigenous spiritual traditions and ways of life. In contemplating the relationship between humans and the greater-than-human world, Kimmerer writes, "The breath of plants gives life to animals and the breath of animals gives life to plants. My breath is your breath, your breath is mine. It's the great poem of give and take, of reciprocity that animates the world."[11]

In the natural world, reciprocity is necessary for life to thrive. It is the way of things—the endless give and take of nature, the changing of the seasons, the passing of day to night, the beginning of one life and the loss of another. Reciprocity has cosmic dimensions, as if the universe continually seeks balance. It's a beautiful thing, and when you have a relationship with an animal that's grounded in reciprocity, it can change your life.

Generosity and gratitude are key aspects of reciprocal relationships.

It all begins with a gift. As discussed here, the best gift we can give to our animal friends is our commitment to understanding their needs as fully as possible and meeting them as best we can. We can also give them the freedom to be themselves. So what can we give to each other? How can we cultivate mutually beneficial relationships with each other so we can grow and thrive?

## Building Networks of Mutual Support

In chapter 6, we explored the social disenfranchisement experienced by people who love animals and grieve their loss. Disenfranchisement is common among pet keepers, but this is beginning to change. In fact, the pet-keeping community is becoming so prominent and its members so outspoken that the pendulum of social belonging and alienation is starting to swing in the other direction.

People who don't keep pets sometimes find themselves surrounded by pet enthusiasts who assume that they, too, love animals. An acquaintance told me that when his family's dog died, his neighbors assumed he and his wife would immediately get another dog. But the dog had belonged to his grown children, and he was looking forward to not having to care for an animal as he entered retirement. He felt judged by his neighbors, as if something were wrong with him for not wanting to have an animal in his life.

Some people who are passionate about animals avoid associating with people who don't share their passion. A woman who participated in my veterinary chaplaincy course was forthcoming about her feelings on this topic. "I've always struggled with having family members and close friends who aren't 'pet people,'" she remarked. "I've always been close with my parents, but they just don't get why my sisters and I love our animals so much. It's almost to the point where that alone can threaten to sever my connection with them, though I know it never would. I can accept pretty much any fault of another person . . . having the so-called wrong political beliefs, or the egregious mistakes they've made, etc. But there's just something about not caring much for animals that I can't get over, and I know other pet people who feel the same way."

Keeping a pet has become so popular, especially among young adults, that it has escalated into a new social currency, or what is aptly described as "pet social networking."[12] Online pet groups offer many benefits for their members. In *One Nation Under Dog*, author Michael Schaffer tells the story of a member of a Chihuahua group in New York City. The woman received more than one hundred emails and telephone calls from her online group when her dog Crystal died. "People who I didn't even know knew me," she said. "They called, and people have sent me cards and brought me gifts—someone brought an urn, and they took her pictures and blew them up. I didn't think I could have gotten through it without all these people."[13]

Pet keepers are also learning to respond to those who question or belittle their love for animals from a place of pride rather than shame. My friend Kim McCool told me about an interaction that speaks to this shift. Kim had been dreaming of starting a pet ministry at her church and had enrolled in my veterinary chaplaincy course as a first step. When she shared her dream with her fellow congregants, some laughed at the idea. One woman told her that the idea of sending a sympathy card to someone who'd lost a pet was the most ridiculous thing she'd ever heard of.

"I'd heard things like this from others, and it hurt me," Kim said. "It made me feel belittled and silly. I could feel myself shut down in those moments. But this time my response was calm and kind. I told this woman that sending a sympathy card can mean the world to someone who has lost a pet. I shared that I still had the sympathy cards from past pet losses and that one loss had just about gutted me. Truthfully, I expected this woman to argue with me or be defensive. Instead, I could see her face change—like she'd had an 'aha!' moment. She became thoughtful and said, 'I'd never thought about that before.

My friend just had to have her horse put to sleep. I should have been more sensitive to her feelings.'"

Stories like this give me hope that people who love animals will continue to find creative ways to support each other. In *Heart Animals*, the first book in the learning series, I introduced the idea that storytelling is the primary way that humans make meaning of their lives. I want to emphasize the importance of this concept because the stories we tell about our animal companions today will help shape how we think about animals in our society in the years to come.

Our stories reflect our experience of the world and simultaneously shape our perceptions of it. As noted earlier, we've inherited one story about animals, but we're beginning to tell a new story that's shaped, in part, by our personal interactions with our pets. I firmly believe that our pet stories make it possible for love to quietly win the day and for more people to begin regarding all animals and the natural world with greater compassion and respect. When someone bears witness to your story of loving and losing an animal, they may be less inclined to think that your dog or your cat is "just an animal." When we learn to speak our truth about animals, people who don't understand what all the fuss is about might just listen.

Pet chaplaincy is an integral part of the vast changes taking place in our spiritual lives. What we hold to be sacred has radical implications for how we conduct ourselves in the world and the choices we make in our lives. When animals, all life on earth, and the earth itself become sacred to us, when we welcome animals and the earth into our spiritual stories, when we regard all living things with reverence rather than mere curiosity or a demand for usefulness, then perhaps we will be inspired to treat animals and the earth with greater care.

Because our society lacks a well-organized support system for pet loss, it has fallen to everyday people to find creative ways to support one another. Building a network of mutual aid may seem daunting, but in my view, it's a great opportunity. This is one of the reasons I created the Pet Chaplain Learning Series. The more people I can reach with this message, the more likely it is that they'll find the courage to share their stories about the animals who've changed their lives. In turn, if I can empower more people to learn to listen to each other's stories with an open mind and heart, the more likely they are to find common ground and improve our lives and the lives of the animals we love.

CHAPTERS 10–12

# Discussion Questions

1.  Chapter 10 described how a close relationship with a pet can change our perception of animals. Tell a story about your own experience or the experience of someone you know whose beliefs about animals changed after experiencing a fulfilling relationship with an animal companion.

2.  The "pets as ambassadors theory" discussed in chapter 10 holds that a close relationship with a pet can promote positive attitudes toward animals and the natural world. Do you believe this is true based on your personal experiences? Why or why not?

3.  Chapter 11 reviewed some ways pet keepers honor the animals they've lost, such as interring them in pet cemeteries and holding memorial services. Describe your own experience honoring an animal you've lost or the experience of someone you know.

4.  In chapter 12, I offered my personal reflections on the challenges we may encounter in the future as the human-animal bond continues to evolve. What changes would you like to see for people and animals in the future? How can you imagine contributing personally to the changes you envision?

# The Sacred Story Project

# Crafting Your Sacred Story: Communicating with Others

The concept of the sacred story was introduced in *Heart Animals*, the first book in the Pet Chaplain Learning Series. A sacred story is a personal narrative that speaks to your deeply held values and beliefs and your sense of meaning and purpose. The goal of crafting a sacred story about your relationship with animals is to explore some fundamental questions: What are your core values and beliefs about animals and the natural world? How have your experiences with animals and the people in your life shaped these values and beliefs? What sparked your interest in the learning series, and what are your hopes for your future in relationship with animals and your fellow human beings?

The sacred story project is a progressive writing exercise, and installments appear in each book in the series. The exercise presented here is the third round of the sacred story project and invites you to focus on your social experiences around the loss of a special pet. If you've completed the first two rounds of the sacred story project, you can integrate the story or stories you've already composed with the story you write here. Alternatively, you might choose to write about a different topic.

Whatever approach you take, be sure to include any spiritual experiences related to the relationship or experience you've chosen to write about. Therapist Pamela A. Hays describes significant spiritual events as "shimmering moments," and this simple phrase captures the unique quality of the experiences that demand our attention and evoke feelings of awe and wonder.[1] Your reflections might include spiritual experiences concerning your pet during their lifetime and following their loss, such as dreams that were particularly memorable or prescient; moments of inexplicable synchronicity; times when you felt a particularly strong sense of awe through a sacred connection with your pet; an occasion when you sensed your deceased pet's physical presence; and prayers, rituals, and other activities you engaged in following their loss that you consider to be sacred.

If you haven't completed the first and second rounds of the sacred story project, you can still complete this exercise. You might wish to expand your story beyond your social experiences to include other aspects of the relationship you've chosen to write about, such as your sense of connection to a pet, the circumstances of their loss, the strategies you used to cope with your grief, and the lessons you learned from that experience. Because the learning series is focused on pet keeping and loss, I encourage you to write a pet who was particularly important to you. But you can write about any relationship or experience you feel is relevant to your spiritual development and identity. The goal of the learning series is, in part, to help you appreciate your connection with the greater-than-human world. Many people who love animals and grieve their loss also grieve the rapid loss of flora and fauna in the modern age. If you feel moved to write about a champion tree and the grief you felt when it was cut down, then please do so. You also might write about the people in your life, particularly if they influenced your relationship with animals.

I recommend holding onto the story or stories you compose now for later use. For those of you who plan to read *Veterinary Chaplaincy*, the next book in the series, you'll have the opportunity to pull everything you've written for the sacred story project into a clear statement of your calling to this new field of spiritual care.

Revisiting your memories of a lost loved one is not an easy task, so it's important to practice good self-care during this process. Be gentle with yourself as you work on your sacred story. Cry or rage when you need to, and allow yourself to feel your feelings. Keep a journal and note whatever arises for you. Practice good self-care by getting plenty of rest, eating healthfully, and exercising. If you feel upset or anxious, take a walk, listen to your favorite music, engage in a relaxing hobby, write in your journal, pray, or meditate—whatever works for you. Above all, I encourage you to reach out to supportive family, friends, or a professional caregiver if you need to share your thoughts and feelings during this process.

This exercise is grounded in writing practice, but feel free to make it your own. You can explore your story in other creative ways that complement your written work. If you're crafty, you could create a scrapbook of photos and other memorabilia related to your chosen topic. Videos, slide shows, and music are great mediums for capturing our experiences and sharing them with others. Compose a poem or prayer, or create a ritual to honor your lost loved one. Do what feels right for you.

## Writing Prompts

The following prompts might give you some inspiration for your story about your social experiences. These prompts concern a pet but can be adapted to whatever it is you've chosen to write about. I also recommend reviewing your answers to the discussion questions presented throughout this book.

- Describe the quality of your social experiences both during your pet's lifetime and after they were lost. Describe interactions that felt supportive to you as well as those that felt unsupportive.

- How did the support you received after losing your loved one help or hinder your ability to cope?
- What lessons did you learn about yourself from these interactions, and what lessons did you learn about the people you interacted with?
- What insights did you gain into who you are as an individual and what you value?
- How did your life change because of the social experiences you've described here?

## Writing Guidelines, Tips, and Suggestions

If you'd like some help getting started or feel stuck at any point in your writing process, the following guidelines, tips, and exercises may be helpful. These also appear in *Heart Animals* and *Always in My Heart*, the first and second books in the learning series, respectively. If you've already read those books and completed the first and second rounds of the sacred story project, you can skip this material.

### Define your guiding purpose

Establishing an overall goal for your narrative can give you some direction. For example, if you'd like to explore your experiences as a pet keeper, you might write about one or two special pets. If you're an animal caregiver who works in the veterinary field or animal rescue, you might focus on the relationships and experiences that compelled you to enter your field. If you're interested in the practice of veterinary chaplaincy, you might consider all the relationships and experiences that have brought you to this book. You can then pull all this work together to create a clear, focused statement about your interest in interfaith spiritual care for pet loss.

## Do some brainstorming

If you have trouble deciding what to write about, I suggest making a list of all the relationships and events that you believe have shaped your love of animals and, if you'd like, your interest in the practice of veterinary chaplaincy. Your list might include interactions with special pets, the important people in your life, memorable experiences in nature, significant milestones in your spiritual life, and so on. The entries on your list do not need to be lengthy descriptions but should include as much detail as you need to make sense of them later. This list provides an at-a-glance summary of the significant relationships and events you might want to write about.

Next, select a single entry from this list that rises above all the others in significance and make three additional lists about that particular relationship or event. These lists should include your reflections on the significance of that relationship, how you coped with the loss of your loved one, and your social experiences surrounding their loss. The goal is to jot down every shimmering moment you can recall about your chosen topic and the thoughts and feelings associated with those memories. You can add to these lists at any time and use them as a reference when composing your story or stories.

Alternatively, you could create a chronological timeline that includes the same information described here. A timeline can help you reconstruct your memory of key events in your life and see them in relation to one another. It's a great way to get a snapshot of the significant milestones of your spiritual journey thus far.

## Some thoughts on revisiting your past

A common bit of wisdom shared by people working on their memoirs is to write from the scar, not the open wound. Time tends to buffer our strong emotions, and we can generally gain a fresh perspective on our losses when our most intense grief has eased. By examining your losses and other life-changing events after some time has passed, you'll be better able to articulate the lessons they hold for you. You'll also be better able to attend to others with the knowledge you've gained from self-reflection, which is particularly important if you're interested in chaplaincy. In the words of Buddhist author Lodro Rinzler, "Once [our] wound has scarred over, we are in fact the best people to talk to others about how to heal from similar situations, because we have been there and learned from it. We know the pain of that wound well and can hold space for other people to be present to it, without judgment."[2]

If you decide to write about a pet, your instinct might be to choose one you've recently lost, especially if that pet was very important to you. However, it might be best to select a pet who was lost at least three months ago. When I interviewed the vet tech students for my doctoral research, they were required to discuss pets they'd lost at least one year before their interview. The powerful meanings they shared with me likely took many months, if not years, to emerge. Many people who've lost pets in childhood or young adulthood were never given the opportunity to unpack those losses, and a great deal of personal insight and growth can be gained by revisiting them. If you want help reconstructing your memories, consider talking with family members or others who knew you and your pet.

### Get visual

Visual aids can be helpful throughout the writing process. If you've chosen to write about a pet, looking at pictures or videos of your animal can help jog your memory. As noted earlier, if your pet was recently lost, you might find that you're overwhelmed with grief when you look at pictures or revisit your memories. This is natural and normal. Even joyful moments can be difficult to revisit when your loss is fresh and your grief intense. Again, be sure to practice good self-care during this process.

### Write from your heart

In the book *Writing Down Your Soul*, author Janet Conner asserts that writing is one of the best ways to make meaning of our experiences and connect with what she calls the "Divine Voice" of wisdom and understanding that resides in all of us.[3] "There is a Voice inside you," Connor writes. "There is a Voice inside everyone. Whether you hear it or not, the Voice is there. Whether you ask for help or ignore its guidance, the Voice is still there. Waiting. It is waiting for you to stop, if just for a moment, and listen. The Voice is always there, guiding you, encouraging you, loving you."[4]

The sacred story project can help you connect with your voice or, as Conner phrases it, "penetrate the thin wall of consciousness that keeps you apart" from your inner voice.[5] Other activities can help you connect with your voice, including prayer, meditation, time spent in nature, and creative work such as the visual arts, music, and dance. But research has shown that there's something unique about the way our brains are wired that makes writing especially effective for new learning and meaning-making.[6]

If writing is difficult for you or you worry that you're not a good writer, your story might flow better when you describe your experiences out loud. Many recording and transcription tools are available to help you quickly convert your spoken story into written form. Remember, too, that your sacred story doesn't have to be perfect. Relax, let your words flow, avoid editing your story as you go, and see what arises. You might be surprised at what emerges if you release the "Divine Voice" within.

### Immerse yourself in a single moment in time

A good way to jump-start your writing process and tap into your divine inner voice is to focus on a single memory that is particularly meaningful to you. You can then expand your story from there. If you're writing about a pet, this might be the occasion when someone was particularly sympathetic and helpful after you lost your pet. Alternatively, you could focus on an interaction with someone that was especially stressful or difficult.

The following immersive writing exercise is designed to focus your attention on a specific time and place and put yourself in the scene. I used this method when composing my sacred story about my dog, Queenie, which appears in *Heart Animals*. It proved to be a powerful way to engage with my past, especially because Queenie died when I was very young.

In brief, you'll write continuously for a set length of time without stopping. I suggest starting with a half hour to see how it feels, but you can shorten this time to fifteen or twenty minutes if you wish. As you write, it's essential to turn off your inner critic. Don't worry about grammar, punctuation, or the organization of your story. If you're writing by hand, don't lift your pen or pencil from the page. Let your mind relax, and your thoughts and feelings flow. Write down whatever comes into your mind, even if it seems repetitive or off topic.

To begin the exercise, find a comfortable place to work, free from distractions and interruptions. I suggest muting your cell phone or leaving it in another room. Set a timer, take some deep breaths, relax your body, close your eyes for a moment, and bring your selected memory to mind. Begin by writing about the physical sensations that you experienced in that moment. Where are you? What things do you see around you? What time of day is it? What season is it? What do you see, hear, taste, and smell? What do you feel on your skin? Is it hot, warm, cool, or cold where you are? Is the wind blowing? Are there others there with you? What happened? Be sure to describe the emotions you experienced as your story unfolds. Were you happy, sad, angry, elated, lonely, or some other feeling, or did you experience a mixture of emotions? When the time is up, take a break, then review what you've written and make any edits you feel are necessary for clarity and narrative flow.

### Wrapping it up

After completing a draft of your story, you might decide that you're happy with it and feel no need to change it. That's absolutely fine. I've found, however, that the editing process can be a learning experience in and of itself. As you review what you've written, other memories, thoughts, and feelings may arise, offering new insights into the connections between your past relationships and experiences and who you are today. It can also be helpful to set your story aside for a while and return to it later. The stories we tell about our past lives are always evolving as we experience new things and engage in new relationships. They're a part of who we are, and I hope this exercise has helped you see your past experiences and yourself in a new way.

Remember, too, that the stories you tell about the animals you've known are their stories as well. We speak on our animals' behalf, and it can be deeply fulfilling to find creative ways to express the gratitude we hold in our hearts for them. Our love for them never dies, and this love can serve as a beacon that guides us to a deeper connection with each other, other animals, and the natural world.

# Our Journey Continues

I invite you to continue your journey with me in the next book in the Pet Chaplain Learning Series, *Veterinary Chaplaincy: Interfaith Spiritual Care for Pet Loss*. My approach to chaplaincy is grounded in storytelling, and with sufficient training and practice, I believe almost everyone has the capacity to offer spiritual support to someone grieving the loss of a pet. The surprising beauty and power of chaplaincy is that, by accompanying others on their grief journey, we may find insight and healing for ourselves. Spiritual care can benefit the caregiver as much as the receiver. The spiritual openness and intentional listening skills that are central to chaplaincy practice can permeate all aspects of our lives, strengthening our sense of loving connection with others and deepening our ability to embrace the suffering that is an unavoidable part of life.

# Acknowledgments

Many acquaintances, friends, and colleagues have contributed to the creation of the Pet Chaplain Learning Series. First, we'd like to recognize the team of advisors who generously dedicated their time and expertise to this project. Your enthusiasm for our work and unfailing encouragement buoyed our spirits when we felt overwhelmed by the vast scope of this project. A big thanks to Rev. Jayne Helgevold, hospice chaplain and pet foster mom; Eileen Medeiros, a college English professor and pug enthusiast; Rev. Linda Moore, Episcopal priest, chaplain, and lifelong animal lover; Nancy Osborne, retired hospital chaplain and Clinical Pastoral Education (CPE) supervisor; Fran Prem, who plans and coordinates CPE programs in Australia; and veterinarian Christine Scott. We're especially grateful to Fran for her detailed edits and astute feedback and the extra time and care she put into this project.

We'd also like to applaud the contributions of Kim McCool, who founded a pet ministry at St. John Vianney Catholic Church in Bettendorf, Iowa, shortly after completing our course. Kim is doing amazing things in her community and is truly an inspiration to us.

The learning series would not be what it is today without the input of all the students who participated in our veterinary chaplaincy course. Thank you to those who agreed to let us include your stories and reflections, and we'd like to give an extra big shout-out to Bob Coulson, Mary DeRosa, and Cindi Rodriguez as well as North Carolina artist Amy Wald for interviewing with us. By graciously allowing us to share your stories with our readers, you've had a positive ripple effect on all the people who will recognize themselves in your tales. And, of course, the learning series might not exist at all without the vet tech students who shared their stories with us. Their moving tales about your heart animals were the spark that compelled us to create the series.

In addition, we'd like to recognize the contributions of two scholars who are experts in the work of cultural anthropologist Ernest Becker, whose ideas about death anxiety are discussed in the third and fourth books in the series: Daniel J. Liechty, emeritus professor of social work at Indiana State University in Terre Haute, Indiana; and Sheldon Solomon, professor of psychology at Skidmore College in Saratoga Springs, New York.

A big thanks to our family and friends who cheered us on over the years; your interest and encouragement mean the world to us. Thanks also to our friend Nancy Rogers for providing a final proofread on the books. We're especially indebted to our friend Larry Robinson. Larry, far too often, we ended up bending your ear as we mulled over the many decisions we needed to make in creating an online course followed by a book series. Your stalwart support and friendship—and the many fine dinners we enjoyed in your company—helped sustain us through this challenging journey.

Finally, and most important of all, we'd like to thank the many animals who've touched our lives and helped us become better people.

# About the Authors

Rob Gierka holds a bachelor's degree in rhetoric and communications from Albany State University, a master's degree in technical writing from Rensselaer Polytechnic Institute, and a doctoral degree in professional and continuing adult education from North Carolina State University with a research focus on the human-animal bond and pet loss. Professionally, Rob enjoyed an eclectic career in communications, serving in various positions in private and public institutions before retiring in June 2016. He got his start in chaplaincy in the early 1990s when he took an extended unit of Clinical Pastoral Education at Rex Hospital in Raleigh, North Carolina, where he subsequently served as a volunteer chaplain for two years. While in training, Rob also served for a year as a Stephen Minister and for three years as chair of the congregational care committee at Pullen Baptist Church in Raleigh. In 2004, he launched the Pet Chaplain organization and began providing interfaith spiritual support to pet keepers in his community. Between 2004 and 2006, he served as the on-call chaplain at the Veterinary Teaching Hospital at North Carolina State University, and in 2006 he launched a pet loss support group at the Raleigh location of the Society for the Prevention of Cruelty to Animals. For five years starting in 2018, Rob co-developed and co-facilitated an online course in veterinary chaplaincy in partnership with his life partner and coauthor Karen Duke.

Karen Duke holds a bachelor's degree in English from the University of Florida. She enjoyed a successful career as a writer and graphic designer before retiring in October 2021 and devoting her talents to the development of the learning series.

# Notes

## Introduction

1. Thomas Kuhn, *The Structure of Scientific Revolutions*, 4th Edition (University of Chicago Press, 2012).

2. David Foster Wallace, *This is Water: Some Thoughts, Delivered on a Significant Occasion, About Living a Compassionate Life* (Little, Brown and Company, 2009), 3.

3. Paulo Freire, *Pedagogy of the Oppressed* (The Continuum International Publishing Group Inc., 1970).

4. Will Durant, *Fallen Leaves: Last Words on Life, Love, War, and God* (Simon & Schuster, 2014), 44.

## Chapter 1: A Tale of Two Rabbits

1. Margo DeMello and Susan E. Davis, *Stories Rabbits Tell: A Natural and Cultural History of a Misunderstood Creature* (Lantern Books, 2003).

2. Margo DeMello and Susan E. Davis, *Stories Rabbits Tell*, 240, Kindle.

3. Alice Villalobos, "Universal Human-Animal Bond Scale," Animal Health Foundation, 2011, https://www.animalhealthfoundation.org/downloads/HAB%20Scale.pdf.

4. Marilyn J. Kwong and Kim Bartholomew, "'Not Just a Dog': An Attachment Perspective on Relationships with Assistance Dogs," *Attachment & Human Development* 13, no. 5 (2011): 421–436, https://doi.org/10.1080/14616734.2011.584410.

5. Margo DeMello, *Animals and Society: An Introduction to Human-Animal Studies* (Columbia University Press, 2012), 157, Kindle.

6. Margo DeMello, *Animals and Society*, 29, Kindle.

7. Dave Aftandilian, Barbara R. Ambros, and Aaron Gross, eds., *Animals and Religion* (Taylor & Francis), 117, Kindle.

8. Victoria C. Krings, Kristof Dhont, and Alina Salmen, "The Moral Divide Between High- and Low-Status Animals: The Role of Human Supremacy Beliefs," *Anthrozoös* 34, no. 6 (2021): 787–802, https://doi.org/10.1080/08927936.2021.1926712.

9. Victoria C. Krings, Kristof Dhont, and Alina Salmen, "The Moral Divide Between High- and Low-Status Animals," 799.

10. Ruth Beatson, Stephen Loughnan, and Michael Halloran, "Attitudes toward Animals: The Effect of Priming Thoughts of Human-Animal Similarities and Mortality Salience on the Evaluation of Companion Animals," *Society and Animals* 17, no. 1 (2009): 72–89, http://dx.doi.org/10.1163/156853009X393774.

11. Victoria C. Krings, Kristof Dhont, and Alina Salmen, "The Moral Divide Between High- and Low-Status Animals," 799.

12. Lynne M. Jackson, "Speciesism Predicts Prejudice Against Low-Status and Hierarchy Attenuating Human Groups," *Anthrozoös* 32, no. 4 (2019): 445–458, https://doi.org/10.1080/08927936.2019.1621514.

13. Yi-Fu Tuan, *Dominance and Affection: The Making of Pets* (Yale University Press, 1984).

14. Yi-Fu Tuan, *Dominance and Affection*, 2.

15. Yi-Fu Tuan, *Dominance and Affection*, 108.

## Chapter 2: A Mutually Beneficial Relationship?

1. PetPartners, "Our Mission & Impact: Human-Animal Therapeutic Bonds," https://petpartners.org/about/.

2. American Veterinary Medical Association, "Human-Animal Bond," https://www.avma.org/one-health/human-animal-bond#:~:text=The%20 human%2Danimal%20bond%20is,%2C%20animals%2C%20and%20the%20 environment.

3. Lisa Beck and Elizabeth A. Madresh, "Romantic Partners and Four-Legged Friends: An Extension of Attachment Theory to Relationships with Pets," *Anthrozoös* 21, no. 1 (2008), 43–56, https://doi.org/10.2752/089279308X274056.

4. Pearl Salotto, ed., *Pet Assisted Therapy: A Loving Intervention and an Emerging Profession* (D.J. Publications, 2001).

5. Froma Walsh, "Human-Animal Bonds II: The Role of Pets in Family Systems and Family Therapy," *Family Process* 48, no. 4 (2009): 482, http://dx.doi. org/10.1111/j.1545-5300.2009.01297.x.

6. Roxanne D. Hawkins, Emma L. Hawkins, and Liesbeth Tip, "'I Can't Give Up When I Have Them to Care for': People's Experiences of Pets and Their Mental Health," *Anthrozoös* 34, no. 4 (2021): 543–562, https://doi.org/10.1080/0892793 6.2021.1914434.

7. Daisy Yuhas, "The Psychology of Pets," *Scientific American MIND*, May/June 2015, 32.

8. Annett Schirmer, Ilona Croy, and Rochelle Ackerley, "What Are C-tactile Afferents and How Do They Relate to 'Affective Touch'?," *Neuroscience & Biobehavioral Reviews* 151 (2023), https://doi.org/10.1016/j. neubiorev.2023.105236.

9.  Céline Brusa and Michèle Bourton, "Candide's Innovative Teaching Method Including Purring Therapy," International Conference on Advanced Research in Education, March 2019, https://www.dpublication.com/wp-content/uploads/2019/03/EDUCATIONCONF-1-136.pdf.

10.  Céline Brusa and Michèle Bourton, "Candide's Innovative Teaching Method Including Purring Therapy."

11.  Adnan I. Qureshi et al., "Cat Ownership and the Risk of Fatal Cardiovascular Diseases: Results from the Second National Health and Nutrition Examination Study," *Journal of Vascular and Interventional Neurology* 2, no. 1 (2009): 132–135, https://pubmed.ncbi.nlm.nih.gov/22518240/.

12.  Charles Siebert, "What Does a Parrot Know About PTSD?" *New York Times Magazine*, January 31, 2016, https://www.nytimes.com/2016/01/31/magazine/what-does-a-parrot-know-about-ptsd.html.

13.  Charles Siebert, "What Does a Parrot Know About PTSD?"

14.  Nicolas Guéguen and Serge Ciccotti, "Domestic Dogs as Facilitators in Social Interaction: An Evaluation of Helping and Courtship Behaviors," *Anthrozoös* 21, no. 4 (2008): 339–349, http://dx.doi.org/10.2752/175303708X371564.

15.  American Pet Products Association, "2017–2018 APPA National Pet Owners Survey," accessed January 6, 2023, https://www.almendron.com/tribuna/wp-content/uploads/2018/06/gpe2017-npos-seminar.pdf.

16.  American Psychiatric Association, "Americans Note Overwhelming Positive Mental Health Impact of Their Pets in New Poll; Dogs and Cats Equally Beneficial," March 1, 2023, https://www.psychiatry.org/news-room/news-releases/positive-mental-health-impact-of-pets.

17.  American Animal Hospital Association, "American Animal Hospital Association 2004 Pet Owner Survey: Summary of Results," accessed October 14, 2024, https://faunalytics.org/wp-content/uploads/2015/05/Citation1058.pdf.

18.  Kristyn R. Vitale, Alexandra Behnke, and Monique A. R. Udell, "Attachment Bonds between Domestic Cats and Humans," *Current Biology* 29, no. 18 (2019): 864–865, https://doi.org/10.1016/j.cub.2019.08.036.

19.  Margo DeMello, *Animals and Society: An Introduction to Human-Animal Studies* (Columbia University Press, 2012), 209.

20.  Céline Brusa and Michèle Bourton, "Candide's Innovative Teaching Method Including Purring Therapy," International Conference on Advanced Research in Education, March 2019, https://www.dpublication.com/wp-content/uploads/2019/03/EDUCATIONCONF-1-136.pdf.

21.  James J. Lynch and W. Horsley Gantt, "The Heart Rate Component of the Social Reflex in Dogs: The Conditional Effects of Petting and Person," *Conditional Reflex* 3 (1968): 69–80, https://doi.org/10.1007/bf03001139.

22. Haruyo Hama, Masao Yogo, and Yoshinori Matsuyama, "Effects of Stroking Horses on Both Humans' and Horses' Heart Rate Responses," *Japanese Psychological Research* 38, no. 2 (May 1996): 66–73, https://doi.org/10.1111/j.1468-5884.1996.tb00009.x.

23. Elsie R. Shore, Deanna K. Douglas, and Michelle L. Riley, "What's In It for the Companion Animal? Pet Attachment and College Students' Behaviors Toward Pets," *Journal of Applied Animal Welfare Science* 8, no. 1 (2005): 1–11, https://doi.org/10.1207/s15327604jaws0801_1.

24. Stephanie D. Clark et al., "Physiological State of Therapy Dogs during Animal-Assisted Activities in an Outpatient Setting," *Animals* 10, no. 5 (2020): 819, https://doi.org/10.3390/ani10050819.

25. Lisa Maria Glenk et al., "Therapy Dogs' Salivary Cortisol Levels Vary during Animal-Assisted Interventions," *Animal Welfare* 22, no. 3 (2013): 369–378, http://dx.doi.org/10.7120/09627286.22.3.369.

26. K. Heimlich, "Animal-Assisted Therapy and the Severely Disabled Child: A Quantitative Study," *Journal of Rehabilitation* 67, no. 4 (2001): 48–54.

27. Richard Louv, *Our Wild Calling: How Connecting with Animals Can Transform Our Lives—and Save Theirs* (Algonquin Books, 2020).

28. Richard Louv, *Our Wild Calling*, 128, Kindle.

29. Richard Louv, *Our Wild Calling*, 129, Kindle.

30. E. B. Bartels, *Good Grief: On Loving Pets, Here and Hereafter* (Mariner Books, 2022), Kindle, 46.

31. Linda Lombardi, "Therapy Dogs Work Miracles. But Do They Like Their Jobs?" *National Geographic*, May 1, 2018, https://www.nationalgeographic.com/animals/article/animals-dogs-therapy-health-pets.

32. Amy Johnson, "Could We Be Creating Stress for Therapy Dogs?," Human-Animal Interaction, Section 13 of Division 17 of the American Psychological Association, accessed October 7, 2024, https://apahaib.wordpress.com/2017/04/20/could-we-be-creating-stress-for-therapy-dogs-amy-johnson/.

## Chapter 3: I Am Not an Animal!

1. Frans de Waal, *Are We Smart Enough to Know How Smart Animals Are?* (W. W. Norton & Company, 2016), 27–28, Kindle.

2. *Merriam-Webster Dictionary*, "Animality," https://www.merriam-webster.com/dictionary/animality.

3. Word Hippo, "What Is Another Word for Animality?," https://www.wordhippo.com/what-is/another-word-for/animality.html.

4. Gary Kurz, *Cold Noses at the Pearly Gates: A Book of Hope for Those Who Have Lost a Pet* (Citadel Press, 2013), 130, Kindle.

5. Ernest Becker, *The Denial of Death* (Free Press Paperbacks, 1973).

6. Ernest Becker, *The Denial of Death*, 26.

7. Ernest Becker, *Escape from Evil* (Free Press, 1975), 92.

8. Michael Mountain and Lori Marino, "'I Am Not an Animal!' The Signature Cry of Our Species," The Ernest Becker Foundation, 2016, December 6, 2016, https://www.ernestbecker.org/the-denial-file/i-am-not-an-animal.

9. Sheldon Solomon, Jeff Greenberg, and Tom Pyszczynski, *The Wom at the Core*, 221, Kindle.

10. Melanie Challenger, *How to Be Animal: A New History of What It Means to Be Human* (Penguin, 2021), 172, Kindle

11. Ruth Beatson, Steve Loughnan, and Michael J. Halloran, "Attitudes toward Animals: The Effect of Priming Thoughts of Human-Animal Similarities and Mortality Salience on the Evaluation of Companion Animals," *Society and Animals* 17, no. 1 (2009): 72–89, https://doi.org/10.1163/156853009X393774.

12. Ruth Beatson, Steve Loughnan, and Michael J. Halloran, "Attitudes toward Animals."

13. Yi-Fu Tuan, *Dominance and Affection: The Making of Pets* (Yale University Press, 1984).

14. Daniel J. Liechty, *Transference and Transcendence: Ernest Becker's Contribution to Psychotherapy* (Jason Aronson Inc., 1995), 164.


## Chapter 4: Animals and Western Society: A Brief History of Ideas


1. Richard Tarnas, *Passion of the Western Mind: Understanding the Ideas That Have Shaped Our World View* (Random House Publishing Group, 2011), 61.

2. Saint Thomas Aquinas, *Summa Contra Gentiles* (Benziger Brothers, 1928).

3. The phrase *dominion mandate* and the word *dominionism* have also been used by a 1970s US Christian political movement that advocates for Christian nationalism. However, I am using these terms to refer specifically to the belief that God granted humankind control over animals and the earth.

4. Alexis Grasse, "The Impact of Anthropocentrism on Christian Environmentalism," *Dialogue & Nexus* 3, no. 18 (2016), https://digitalcommons.acu.edu/dialogue/vol3/iss1/18; and Anna L. Peterson, "In and of the World? Christian Theological Anthropology and Environmental Ethics," *Journal of Agricultural and Environmental Ethics* 12, no. 3 (2000): 237–261, https://doi.org/10.1023/A:1009503215606.

5. Lisa Jacks, "7 Mainline Christian Denominations' Stances on Animal Rights," Newsmax, May 6, 2015, https://www.newsmax.com/fastfeatures/christian-animal-rights-mainline-stance/2015/05/06/id/643038/.

6. Colin Jerolmack, "Tracing the Profile of Animal Rights Supporters: A Preliminary Investigation," *Society & Animals* 11, no. 3 (2003), 245–263, https://doi.org/10.1163/156853003322773041; and Jamie L. DeLeeuwa et al., "Support for Animal Rights as a Function of Belief in Evolution, Religious Fundamentalism, and Religious Denomination," *Society & Animals* 15, no. 4 (2007), 353–363, https://doi.org/10.1163/156853007X235528.

7. Jamie L. DeLeeuwa et al., "Support for Animal Rights as a Function of Belief in Evolution, Religious Fundamentalism, and Religious Denomination," 362.

8. Paul Waldau, "Religion and Animals," in *In Defense of Animals*, ed. Peter Singer (Blackwell Publishing, 2006), 82.

9. Lynn White Jr., "The Historical Roots of Our Ecologic Crisis," *Science* 155, no. 3767 (1967): 1203–07, https://doi.org/10.1126/science.155.3767.1203.

10. Matthew Scully, *Dominion: The Power of Man, the Suffering of Animals, and the Call to Mercy* (St. Martin's Press, 2002), xi.

11. Alberto A. Martinez, *Burned Alive: Bruno, Galileo and the Inquisition* (Reaktion Books, 2018).

12. History.com, "Galileo Goes on Trial for Heresy," accessed October 7, 2024, https://www.history.com/this-day-in-history/galileo-is-accused-of-heresy.

13. Dénes Karasszon, *A Concise History of Veterinary Medicine* (Akadémiai Kiadó, 1988), 263.

14. Dénes Karasszon, *A Concise History of Veterinary Medicine*, 269.

15. Stephen Gaukroger, *Descartes: An Intellectual Biography* (Oxford University Press, 1995), 291.

16. John Veitch, *The Method, Meditations and Philosophy of Descartes* (Tudor Publishing Company, 1901), 4.

17. Dénes Karasszon, *A Concise History of Veterinary Medicine*, 269.

18. Carolyn Merchant, *The Death of Nature: Women, Ecology, and the Scientific Revolution*, 40th Anniversary Edition (Harper Collins, 2019).

19. Eshin Nishimura, "Embracing Earth while Facing Death: A Buddhist Monk Reflects on the Limits of Contemporary Science," Harvard Divinity Bulletin, Spring/Summer 2007, https://bulletin.hds.harvard.edu/embracing-earth-while-facing-death/.

20. Rod Preece, "The History of Animal Ethics in Western Culture," in *The Psychology of the Human–Animal Bond: A Resource for Clinicians and Researchers*, eds. Christopher Blazina, Güler Boyraz, and David Shen-Miller (Springer, 2011), 45.

21. Rod Preece, "The History of Animal Ethics in Western Culture," 48.

22. Virginia Morell, *Animal Wise: How We Know Animals Think and Feel* (Broadway Books, 2013) 10, Kindle.

## Chapter 5: Almost Family Members

1. James Serpell, *In the Company of Animals: A Study of Human-Animal Relationships*, 2nd edition (Cambridge University Press, 1996), 25.

2. James A. Serpell, *In the Company of Animals*, 25.

3. John Archer, "Pet Keeping: A Case Study of Maladaptive Behavior," *The Oxford Handbook of Evolutionary Family Psychology* (Oxford University Press, 2011).

4. James A. Serpell, *In the Company of Animals*, 25.

5. Angela Dudley, "199 Animals Removed From Lynnfield Home," Animal Rescue League of Boston, March 10, 2014, https://www.arlboston.org/199-animals/.

6. Iris Smolkovic, Mateja Fajfar, and Vesna Mlinaric, "Attachment to Pets and Interpersonal Relationships," *Journal of European Psychology Students* 3 No. 1 (2012): 21, https://doi.org/10.5334/jeps.ao.

7. James A. Serpell, *In the Company of Animals*, 41.

8. Emily Leonhardt-Parr and Benjamin Rumble, "Coping with Animal Companion Loss: A Thematic Analysis of Pet Bereavement Counselling," *OMEGA Journal of Death and Dying* 89. no. 1 (2022): 12, https://doi.org/10.1177/00302228211073217.

9. Bianca F. Lavorgna and Vicki E. Hutton, "Grief Severity: A Comparison Between Human and Companion Animal Death," *Death Studies* 43, no. 8 (2019): 521–526, https://doi.org./10.1080/07481187.2018.1491485.

10. Bianca F. Lavorgna and Vicki E. Hutton, "Grief Severity," 526.

11. Patricia Fersch, "Is Your Pet a Piece of Property or a Beloved Family Member?" *Forbes*, January 15, 2024, https://www.forbes.com/sites/patriciafersch/2024/01/15/is-your-pet-a-piece-of-property-or-a-beloved-family-member/?sh=1d95cf435bbd.

12. For additional information on the animal protection laws for every state in the US, visit the website of the Animal Legal Defense Fund (ALDF) at aldf.org.

13. Patricia Fersch, "Is Your Pet a Piece of Property or a Beloved Family Member?"

14. Arnold Arluke, *Just a Dog: Understanding Animal Cruelty and Ourselves* (Temple University Press, 2001), Introduction, Kindle.

15. Melissa M. Kelley, *Grief Transition and Loss: Contemporary Theory and the Practice of Ministry* (Fortress Press, 2010), 15.

16. Mark L. Cushing, *Pet Nation: The Love Affair that Changed America* (Avery, 2020), 32, Kindle.

17.  American Pets Products Association, "Industry Trends and Stats," accessed October 7, 2024, https://americanpetproducts.org/industry-trends-and-stats.

18.  Jessica Pierce, *Run, Spot, Run: The Ethics of Keeping Pets* (The University of Chicago Press, 2016).

19.  Jessica Pierce, *Run, Spot, Run*, 4, Kindle.

20.  Shawn Ashley et al., "Morbidity and Mortality of Invertebrates, Amphibians, Reptiles, and Mammals at a Major Exotic Companion Animal Wholesaler," *Journal of Applied Animal Welfare Science* 17, no. 4 (2014): 308–321, https://doi.org/10.1080/10888705.2014.918511.

21.  Mary Shannon Johnstone, "Landfill Dogs," https://landfilldogs.com/about/. The book is no longer available.

22.  Sarah Weir and Sharon E. Kessler, "The Making of a (Dog) Movie Star: The Effect of the Portrayal of Dogs in Movies on Breed Registrations in the United States," *PLoS One* 17, no. 1 (2022), https://doi.org/10.1371/journal.pone.0261916.

23.  Daisy Yuhas, "The Psychology of Pets," *Scientific American MIND*, May/June 2015, 31.

24.  Daisy Yuhas, "The Psychology of Pets," Scientific American MIND, May/June 2015, 31.

25.  Michelle Megna, "54% of Dog Owners Have Regrets About Getting a Dog," *Forbes Advisor*, December 8, 2022, https://www.forbes.com/advisor/pet-insurance/survey-pet-ownership-regret-dog/.

26.  Hope M. Tiesman et al., "Suicide in U.S. Workplaces, 2003–2010: A Comparison with Non-Workplace Suicides," *American Journal of Preventative Medicine* 48, no. 6 (2015): 674–682, https://doi.org/10.1016/j.amepre.2014.12.011.

## Chapter 6: The Lonely Journey of Pet Loss

1.  Tatiana Gallardo, "I Hate Dogs and I Am Not a Horrible Human Being," *The Fordham Observer*, November 7, 2018, https://fordhamobserver.com/36084/opinions/i-hate-dogs-and-i-am-not-a-horrible-human-being/.

2.  Caroline Knapp, *Pack of Two: The Intricate Bond Between People and Dogs* (Random House, 2010), 9.

3.  Kenneth Doka, *Disenfranchised Grief: Recognizing Hidden Sorrow* (Lexington Books, 1989).

4.  Rachel Park and Kenneth Royal, "A National Survey of Companion Animal Owners' Self-Reported Methods of Coping Following Euthanasia," *Veterinary Science* 7, no. 3 (2020): 89, https://doi.org/10.3390/vetsci7030089.

5.  Kelly A. McCutcheon and Stephen J. Fleming, "Grief Resulting from Euthanasia and Natural Death of Companion Animals," *Omega* 44, (2002): 169–188, https://doi.org/10.2190/5QG0-HVH8-JED0-ML16.

6.  Lillian Tzivian, Michael Friger, and Talma Kushnir, "Grief and Bereavement of Israeli Dog Owners: Exploring Short-Term Phases Pre- and Post-Euthanization," *Death Studies* 38 (2014): 109–117, https://doi.org/10.1080/07481187.2012.73876 4.

7.  Christina Michael and Mick Cooper, "Post-Traumatic Growth Following Bereavement: A Systematic Review of the Literature," *Counseling Psychology Review* 28 (2013): 18–33, http://dx.doi.org/10.53841/bpscpr.2013.28.4.18.

8.  Naomi I. Eisenberger, Matthew D. Lieberman, and Kipling D. Williams, "Does Rejection Hurt? An fMRI Study of Social Exclusion," *Science* 302, no. 10 (2003): 290–292, https://www.science.org/doi/10.1126/science.1089134.

9.  Cori Bussolari et al., "Self-Compassion, Social Constraints, and Psychosocial Outcomes in a Pet Bereavement Sample," *OMEGA Journal of Death and Dying* 82, no. 3 (2021): 389–408, http://dx.doi.org/10.1177/0030222818814050.

10. Kathy Charmaz and Melinda Milligan, "Grief," in *The Handbook of the Sociology of Emotions*, eds. Jan Stets and Jonathan H. Turner (Springer Science & Business Media, 2007).

11. Bianca F. Lavorgna and Vicki E. Hutton, "Grief Severity: A Comparison Between Human and Companion Animal Death," *Death Studies* 43, no. 8 (2019): 525, https://doi.org./10.1080/07481187.2018.1491485.

12. Michelle Cleary et al., "Grieving the Loss of a Pet: A Qualitative Systematic Review," *Death Studies* 46, no. 9 (2022): 2173, https://doi.org/10.1080/07481187. 2021.1901799.


## Chapter 7: A Spiritual Void


1.  Pew Research Center, "How U.S. Religious Composition Has Changed in Recent Decades," September 13, 2022, https://www.pewresearch.org/religion/2022/09/13/how-u-s-religious-composition-has-changed-in-recent-decades/.

2.  Barbara Ambros, "Celebrating Creation and Commemorating Life: Ritualizing Pet Death in the U.S. and Japan," in *The Routledge History of Death Since 1800*, ed. Peter N. Stearns (Taylor & Francis, 2021), 463, Kindle.

Note: Barbara Ambros was on my dissertation committee for my doctoral degree in adult education when I studied the human-animal bond and bereavement. In the chapter cited above, she mentions my work as a pet chaplain, noting that the spiritual void "has in part been filled by the relatively new vocation of pet chaplains, who emerged in the first two decades of the twenty-first century and often draw on an array of religious traditions and pet-loss discourses."

3. Barbara Ambros, "Celebrating Creation and Commemorating Life: Ritualizing Pet Death in the U.S. and Japan," 463, Kindle.

4. Michał Piotr Pręgowski, "Memorial Services and Rituals for Companion Animals in Japan, Poland and the United States of America," *Analecta Nipponica* 8 (2018), 114.

5. Episcopal Church of the United States, "Service at the Loss of a Beloved Animal," *Journal of the 77th General Convention of the Protestant Episcopal Church in the United States of America* (The General Convention of the Episcopal Church, 2012).

6. Sid Korpi, *Good Grief: Finding Peace After Pet Loss* (Healy House Books, 2009).

7. Sid Korpi, *Good Grief*, 293.

8. Sid Korpi, *Good Grief*, 294.

9. Pope Francis, "Encyclical Letter Laudato Si' of the Holy Father Francis on Care for Our Common Home," 2022, https://www.vatican.va/content/francesco/en/encyclicals/documents/papa-francesco_20150524_enciclica-laudato-si.html.

10. Jordan Liles, "Pope Francis on Pets Over Kids: Full Transcript and Video," Snopes, January 6, 2022, https://www.snopes.com/news/2022/01/06/pope-francis-pets-kids/.

11. Kenneth D. Royal, April A. Kedrowicz, and Amy M. Snyder, "Do All Dogs Go to Heaven? Investigating the Association between Demographic Characteristics and Beliefs about Animal Afterlife," *Anthrozoös* 29, no. 3 (2016): 409–20, https://doi.org/10.1080/08927936.2016.1189748.

12. Dalia Sussman, "POLL: See Spot Go to Heaven? The Public's Not So Sure," ABC News, July 20, 2001, https://abcnews.go.com/U.S./PollVault/story?id=3440869.

13. Dalia Sussman, "POLL: See Spot Go to Heaven?"

14. Dalia Sussman, "POLL: See Spot Go to Heaven?"

15. Helen Davis et al., "When a Pet Dies: Religious Issues, Euthanasia and Strategies for Coping with Bereavement," *Anthrozoös* 16, no. 1 (2003): 57–74, https://doi.org/10.2752/089279303786992378.

16. Jake Frandsen, "What Church Leaders Have Actually Said About Animals in Heaven," LDS Living, April 11, 2023, https://www.ldsliving.com/what-church-leaders-have-said-about-animals-in-heaven/s/11217.

17. United Methodist Communications, "How Pets Bless Human Souls," October 1, 2015, https://www.umc.org/en/content/how-pets-bless-human-souls.

18. John Wesley, "The New Creation: Sermon 64, Text from the 1872 Edition," ed. Thomas Jackson, Resource UMC, accessed October 7, 2024, https://www.resourceumc.org/en/content/sermon-64-the-new-creation.

19. Billy Graham Evangelistic Association, June 1, 2004, https://billygraham.org/answer/will-there-be-animals-in-heaven/.

20. Stanley Coren, "Pope Francis Says That All Dogs Go to Heaven," *Psychology Today*, December 10, 2014, https://www.psychologytoday.com/ie/blog/canine-corner/201412/pope-francis-says-all-dogs-go-heaven#:~:text=These%20views%20were%20strongly%20held,into%20heaven%20in%20earlier%20regimes.

21. Rick Gladstone, "Dogs in Heaven? Pope Francis Leaves Pearly Gates Open," *The New York Times*, December 11, 2014, http://www.nytimes.com/2014/12/12/world/europe/dogs-in-heaven-pope-leaves-pearly-gate-open-.html#:~:text=It%20drew%20an%20analogy%20to,to%20all%20of%20God's%20creatures.%E2%80%9D.

22. Shanna Johnson, "All Animals Go to Heaven,"Catholic Voices, February 11, 2016, https://uscatholic.org/blog/a-heaven-for-all/#:~:text=In%201990%20he%20is%20reported,for%20pet%20lovers%20to%20reconcile.

23. Pope Francis, "Encyclical Letter Laudato Si' of the Holy Father Francis on Care for Our Common Home," 2022, https://www.vatican.va/content/francesco/en/encyclicals/documents/papa-francesco_20150524_enciclica-laudato-si.html.

24. Deborah Cornah, *The Impact of Spirituality on Mental Health: A Review of the Literature* (The Mental Health Foundation, 2006), PDF ebook.

25. Andrew Newberg and Mark Robert Waldman, *How God Changes Your Brain: Breakthrough Findings from a Leading Neuroscientist* (Random House, 2010), 149.

26. Kathleen A. Cooney et al., "Pet Owners' Expectations for Pet End-of-Life Support and After-Death Body Care: Exploration and Practical Applications," *Topics in Companion Animal Medicine* 43 (2020), https://doi.org/10.1016/j.tcam.2020.100503.

27. Lori R. Kogan et al., "Pet Death and Owners' Memorialization Choices," *Illness, Crisis & Loss* 32, no. 2 (2022), https://doi.org/10.1177/10541373221143046.

28. Dave Aftandilian, Barbara R. Ambros, and Aaron S. Gross, eds., *Animals and Religion* (Taylor & Francis, 2024), 8, Kindle.

29. Cynthia Bourgeault, *The Wisdom Jesus: Transforming Heart and Mind–A New Perspective on Christ and His Message* (Boston: Shambhala, 2008).

30. Cynthia Bourgeault, *The Wisdom Jesus*, 4, Kindle.

31. Cynthia Bourgeault, *The Wisdom Jesus*, 56, Kindle.

32. Gary Kurz, *Cold Noses at the Pearly Gates: A Book of Hope for Those Who Have Lost a Pet* (Citadel Press, 2013).

33. Gary Kurz, *Cold Noses at the Pearly Gates*, 18, Kindle.

34. Melissa M. Kelley, *Grief Transition and Loss: Contemporary Theory and the Practice of Ministry* (Fortress Press, 2010), 12–13.

35. Episcopal Church of the United States, "Service at the Loss of a Beloved Animal," *Journal of the 77th General Convention of the Protestant Episcopal Church in the United States of America* (The General Convention of the Episcopal Church, 2012).

36. Barbara Ambros, "Celebrating Creation and Commemorating Life: Ritualizing Pet Death in the U.S. and Japan," *The Routledge History of Death Since 1800*, ed. Peter N. Stearns (Taylor & Francis, 2021), 460, Kindle.

37. Barbara Ambros, "Celebrating Creation and Commemorating Life," 470, Kindle.

38. Laura Hobgood, "Blessings of Pets in Jewish and Christian Traditions," in *Animals and Religion*, eds. Dave Aftandilian, Barbara R. Ambros, and Aaron Gross (Taylor & Francis, 2024), 139, Kindle.

39. Laura Hobgood, "Blessings of Pets in Jewish and Christian Traditions," 141, Kindle.

40. Laura Hobgood, "Blessings of Pets in Jewish and Christian Traditions," 141, Kindle.

## Chapter 8: An Evolving Spiritual Narrative About Animals

1. Jeremy Bentham, *An Introduction to the Principles of Morals and Legislation* (Dover Publications, Inc., 2007 [1780]), 311.

2. Anna Sewell, *Black Beauty* (Dover Publications, 1999 [1877]).

3. Richard Louv, *Our Wild Calling: How Connecting with Animals Can Transform Our Lives—and Save Theirs* (Algonquin Books, 2020), 11.

4. Kenneth D. Royal, April A. Kedrowicz, and Amy M. Snyder, "Do All Dogs Go to Heaven? Investigating the Association between Demographic Characteristics and Beliefs about Animal Afterlife," *Anthrozoös* 29, no. 3 (2016): 409–20, https://doi.org/10.1080/08927936.2016.1189748.

5. John Katz, *Soul of a Dog: Reflections on the Spirits of the Animals of Bedlam Farm* (Random House, 2009).

6. John Katz, *Soul of a Dog*, 11, Kindle.

7. John Katz, *Soul of a Dog*, 68, Kindle.

8. Marc Bekoff and Jessica Pierce, *Wild Justice: The Moral Lives of Animals* (University of Chicago Press, 2009).

9. Marc Bekoff and Jessica Pierce, *Wild Justice*, ix. The Arnhem Zoo is commonly known as Burgers' Zoo.

10. Gary Kowalski, *The Souls of Animals* (New World Press, 1999), 23.

11. Benedict de Spinoza, *Ethics*, ed. and trans. Edwin Curley (Penguin Publishing Group, 1996 [1677]).

12. My understanding of Spinoza's work was drawn in part from the novel by psychiatrist Irvin D. Yalom titled *The Spinoza Problem* (Basic Books, 2012).

13. Thomas Berry, *The Great Work: Our Way into the Future* (Crown, 2011), 49.

14. The phrase "ghost in the machine" was coined by Gilbert Ryle, *The Concept of Mind* (Penguin, 2000), xvii. For information on efforts to connect the human brain with computers, see the article titled "Downloading Consciousness" by Jordan Inafuku, Katie Lampert, Brad Lawson, Shaun Stehly, and Alex Vaccaro on the Stanford University website at https://cs.stanford.edu/people/eroberts/cs181/projects/2010-11/DownloadingConsciousness/tandr.html#:~:text=Although%20a%20brief%20examination%20of,certainly%20a%20cause%20for%20hope.

15. John O'Donohue, *Anam Cara: A Book of Celtic Wisdom* (HarperCollins, 1997), 50.

16. Wendell Berry, *The Unsettling of America: Culture and Agriculture* (Sierra Club Books, 1977), 105.

17. Wendell Berry, *The Unsettling of America*, 103.

18. As cited in Andrew Linzey, *Animal Rites: A Christian Assessment of Man's Treatment of Animals* (SCM Press, 1976), 2.

19. Becka A. Alper, "How Religion Intersects With Americans' Views on the Environment," Pew Research Center, November 17, 2022, https://www.pewresearch.org/religion/2022/11/17/how-religion-intersects-with-americans-views-on-the-environment/#:~:text=The%20new%20survey%2C%20conducted%20April,their%20views%20about%20climate%20change.

20. Allison Covey, "Animal Theology," in *Animals and Religion*, eds. Dave Aftandilian, Barbara R. Ambros, and Aaron Gross (Taylor & Francis, 2024), 120, Kindle.

21. Allison Covey, "Animal Theology," 120, Kindle.

22. Andrew Linzey, *Animal Rights: A Christian Assessment of Man's Treatment of Animals* (SCM Press, 1976).

23. Dave Aftandilian, Barbara R. Ambros, and Aaron Gross, eds., *Animals and Religion* (Taylor & Francis), 118, Kindle.

24. Andrew Linzey and Clair Linzey, eds., *Animal Theologians*, (Oxford University Press, 2023), 3–5.

25. Andrew Linzey, *Animal Rites: Liturgies of Animal Care* (Wipf and Stock Publishers, 1999).

26. Andrew Linzey, *Animal Rites*, 3.

27. Matthew Scully, *Dominion: The Power of Man, the Suffering of Animals, and the Call to Mercy* (St. Martin's Press, 2002).

28. Desmond Tutu, foreword to *The Global Guide to Animal Protection*, ed. Andrew Linzey (University of Illinois Press, 2013), xv.

29. Desmond Tutu in *The Global Guide to Animal Protection*, Foreword.

30. William Sloane Coffin, "The Politics of Compassion: The Heart Is a Little to the Left," *Harvard Divinity Bulletin* 28, no. 2–3 (1999): 11–12.

31. Keith Akers, *Disciples: How Jewish Christianity Shaped Jesus and Shattered the Church* (Apocryphile Press, 2013), 9.

32. The Christian Vegetarian Association, accessed October 7, 2024, https://christianveg.org/.

33. "CreatureKind," *Pacific Roots Magazine*, February 26, 2020, https://pacificrootsmagazine.com/creaturekind/.

34. Lisa Kemmerer, *Animals and Christianity* (Tapestry, 2022), 4, Kindle.

## Chapter 9: The New Animal Science

1. Andrew Knight, "Conscientious Objection to Harmful Animal Use Within Veterinary and Other Biomedical Education," *Animals* 4 (2014): 16–34, https://doi.org/10.3390%2Fani4010016.

2. Katherine Mangan, "Can Vet Schools Teach Without Killing Animals?" *The Chronicle of Higher Education*, February 4, 2000, https://www.chronicle.com/article/can-vet-schools-teach-without-killing-animals/.

3. Andrew Knight and Miriam A. Zemanova, "18 Animal Use in Veterinary Education," Veterinary Key, retrieved February 14, 2025, https://veteriankey.com/animal-use-in-veterinary-education/#:~:text=Veterinary%20schools%20that%20have%20eliminated,kill%20animals%20for%20teaching%20purposes.

4. Coco Lederhouse, "AAVMC Publishes Handbook for Use of Animals in Veterinary Education: Recommendations Offered for Veterinary Colleges on Ethically Sourcing Cadavers, Using Animal Models," AVMA News, June 18, 2024, https://www.avma.org/news/aavmc-publishes-handbook-use-animals-veterinary-education#:~:text=Variation%20exists%20among%20use%20of,reported%20using%20no%20live%20animals.

5. Paul Waldau, "Religion and Animals," in *In Defense of Animals*, ed. Peter Singer, (Blackwell Publishing, 2006), 82.

6. Matej Mikulic, "Number of Animals Used in Research and Testing Worldwide 2020 by Country," Statista, September 4, 2023, https://www.statista.com/statistics/639954/animals-used-in-research-experiments-worldwide/#:~:text=In%202020%2C%20the%20United%20States,and%20testing%20in%20that%20year.

7.  Margo DeMello, *Animals and Society: An Introduction to Human-Animal Studies* (Columbia University Press, 2012), 21, Kindle.

8.  Charles Darwin, *On the Origin of Species* (John Wiley & Sons Ltd., 2020 [1859]).

9.  Charles Darwin, *The Descent of Man, and Selection in Relation to Sex*, Vol. 1 (New York: D. Appleton and Company, 1871 [1936]); and Charles Darwin, *The Expression of Emotions in Man and Animals* (Oxford University Press, 1996 [1872]).

10.  Charles Darwin, *The Descent of Man and Selection in Relation to Sex*, 58.

11.  Margo DeMello, *Animals and Society: An Introduction to Human-Animal Studies* (Columbia University Press, 2012), 342, Kindle.

12.  Frans de Waal, *Are We Smart Enough to Know How Smart Animals Are?* (W. W. Norton & Company, 2016), 4, Kindle.

13.  Frans de Waal, *Are We Smart Enough to Know How Smart Animals Are?*, 122, Kindle.

14.  Ernest Becker, *The Denial of Death* (Simon and Schuster, 1973), 84–85, Kindle.

15.  Stephen Budiansky, *If a Lion Could Talk: Animal Intelligence and the Evolution of Consciousness* (Free Press, 1998), 193–194.

16.  Jakob von Uexküll, *Umwelt und Innenwelt der Tiere* (Verlag von Julius Springer, 1909).

17.  Ed Yong, *An Immense World: How Animal Senses Reveal the Hidden Realms Around Us* (Random House, 2022), 6, Kindle.

18.  Virginia Morell, *Animal Wise: How We Know Animals Think and Feel* (Broadway Books, 2013), 23, Kindle.

19.  Jane Goodall in *The Emotional Lives of Animals: A Leading Scientist Explores Animal Joy, Sorrow, and Empathy—and Why They Matter*, Marc Bekoff (New World Library, 2007), xii.

20.  Jane Goodall in *The Emotional Lives of Animals*, xii.

21.  Donald Redfield Griffin, *The Question of Animal Awareness* (Rockefeller University Press, 1976).

22.  Frans de Waal, *Are We Smart Enough to Know How Smart Animals Are?*, 13, Kindle.

23.  Frans de Waal, *Are We Smart Enough to Know How Smart Animals Are?*, 4–5, Kindle.

24.  Marc Bekoff, *The Emotional Lives of Animals*, 30.

25.  Frans de Waal, *Are We Smart Enough to Know How Smart Animals Are?*, 12, Kindle.

26. Hal Herzog, "We Know Animals Have Personalities. Does That Make Them Persons?," *Psychology Today*, June 21, 2021, https://www.psychologytoday.com/us/blog/animals-and-us/202106/we-know-animals-have-personalities-does-make-them-persons.

27. Hal Herzog, "We Know Animals Have Personalities."

28. P. Low, "The Cambridge Declaration on Consciousness. Proceedings of the Francis Crick Memorial Conference," Churchill College, Cambridge University, July 7, 2012, 1, https://fcmconference.org/img/CambridgeDeclarationOnConsciousness.pdf.

29. Marc Bekoff, *The Emotional Lives of Animals*, 32–33.

30. Marc Bekoff, *The Emotional Lives of Animals*, xviii.

31. Marc Bekoff, *The Emotional Lives of Animals*, 113.

32. Marc Bekoff, *The Emotional Lives of Animals*, 46.

33. American Animal Hospital Association, "National Pet Owners Survey," 2015, Accessed October 7, 2024, https://faunalytics.org/wp-content/uploads/2015/05/Citation1058.pdf.

34. Stephanie Gibeault, "How to Read Dog Body Language," American Kennel Club, June 22, 2023, https://www.akc.org/expert-advice/advice/how-to-read-dog-body-language/.

35. Marc Bekoff, *The Emotional Lives of Animals*, 50.

36. Miho Nagasawa, et al., "Oxytocin-Gaze Positive Loop and the Coevolution of Human-Dog Bonds," *Science* 17, no. 348 (April 2015): 333–336, https://doi.org/10.1126/science.1261022.

37. Virginia Morell, *Animal Wise: How We Know Animals Think and Feel* (Crown Publishing, 2013), 1, Kindle.

38. Wayne Purcell, *The Bond: Our Kinship with Animals, Our Call to Defend Them* (Harper Collins, 2011), xiii.

39. Tom Regan in *The Souls of Animals*, Gary Kowalski (New World Library, 1999), 14.

40. Marc Bekoff, *The Emotional Lives of Animals*, 50

41. Marc Bekoff, *The Emotional Lives of Animals*, 24.

## Chapter 10: Across the Rainbow Bridge

1. Paul Koudounaris, "The Rainbow Bridge: The True Story Behind History's Most Influential Piece of Animal Mourning Literature," The Order of the Good Death, February 9, 2023, https://www.orderofthegooddeath.com/article/the-rainbow-bridge-the-true-story-behind-historys-most-influential-piece-of-animal-mourning-literature/.

2. Paul Koudounaris, "The Rainbow Bridge."

3. Paul Koudounaris, "The Rainbow Bridge."

4. Barbara King, "Do Pet Obituaries Belong in the Newspaper?" National Public Radio, April 5, 2012, http://www.npr.org/sections/13.7/2012/04/05/149951712/do-pet-obituaries-belong-in-the-newspaper.

5. Susan Palwick, "Harlequin Palwick Meyer," *Rickety Contrivances of Doing Good*, October 3, 2010, https://improbableoptimisms.blogspot.com/2010/10/harlequin-palwick-meyer.html.

6. Lori R. Kogan et al., "Pet Death and Owners' Memorialization Choices," *Illness, Crisis & Loss* 32, no. 2 (2022), https://doi.org/10.1177/10541373221143046.

7. Kimberly J. Lyons, "Cycles, Ceremonies, and Creeping Phlox," *Journal of Leisure Research* 45, no. 5 (2013): 624–643, https://doi.org/10.18666/jlr-2013-v45-i5-4366.

8. Stanley Brandes, "The Meaning of American Pet Cemetery Gravestones," *Ethnology* 48, no. 2 (2009): 99–118.

9. Stanley Brandes, "The Meaning of American Pet Cemetery Gravestones," 102.

10. E. B. Bartels, *Good Grief: On Loving Pets, Here and Hereafter* (Mariner Books, 2022), xi-xii.

11. E. B. Bartels, *Good Grief*, xi-xii.

12. Best Friends Animal Society, "Welcome to Best Friends Animal Sanctuary," Accessed October 7, 2024, https://bestfriends.org/sanctuary.

13. Helen Davis et al., "When a Pet Dies: Religious Issues, Euthanasia and Strategies for Coping with Bereavement," Anthrozoös 16, no. 1 (2003), 57–74, https://doi.org/10.2752/089279303786992378.

## Chapter 11: Animal Ambassadors

1. Pet Product News, "The American Pet Products Association (APPA) Releases 2025 Dog & Cat Report, Revealing a New Era of Pet Ownership," June 24, 2025, https://americanpetproducts.org/news/the-american-pet-products-association-appa-releases-2025-dog-cat-report.

2. Malinda Larkin, "Pet Population Still on the Rise, with Fewer Pets Per Household," American Veterinary Medical Association, November 17, 2021, https://www.avma.org/javma-news/2021-12-01/pet-population-still-rise-fewer-pets-household.

3. Malinda Larkin, "Pet Population Still on the Rise, with Fewer Pets Per Household."

4. Harris Poll, "More than Ever, Pets Are Members of the Family," Cision PR Newswire, July 16, 2015, https://www.prnewswire.com/news-releases/more-than-ever-pets-are-members-of-the-family-300114501.html.

5. Terry Hartig et al., "Health Benefits of Nature Experience: Psychological, Social and Cultural Processes," in *Forests, Trees and Human Health*, eds. Kjell Nilsson et al. (Springer, 2011): 127–168, https://doi.org/10.1007/978-90-481-9806-1_5.

6. Béatrice Auger and Catherine E. Amiot, "Testing and Extending the Pets as Ambassadors Hypothesis: The Role of Contact with Pets and Recategorization Processes in Predicting Positive Attitudes Toward Animals," *Human-Animal Interaction Bulletin* 5, no. 1 (2017): 1–25, https://doi.org/10.1079/hai.2017.0005.

7. Béatrice Auger and Catherine E. Amiot, "Testing and Extending the Pets as Ambassadors Hypothesis."

## Chapter 12: Animal Dreams

1. Charles Eisenstein, *The More Beautiful World Our Hearts Know Is Possible* (North Atlantic Books, 2013), 55, Kindle.

2. Melanie Challenger, *How to Be Animal: A New History of What It Means to Be Human* (Penguin Books), 1, Kindle.

3. Hannah Ritchie, "Wild Mammals Make Up Only a Few Percent of the World's Mammals," Our World in Data, December 15, 2022, https://ourworldindata. org/wild-mammals-birds-biomass#:~:text=Livestock%20make%20up%20 62%25%20of,wild%20mammals%20are%20just%204%25.

4. Marc Bekoff, *The Emotional Lives of Animals: A Leading Scientist Explores Animal Joy, Sorrow, and Empathy—and Why They Matter* (New World Library, 2010), 24.

5. Martin Buber, *I and Thou* (Scribner, 1958).

6. Abraham H. Maslow, "A Theory of Human Motivation," *Psychological Review* 50, no. 4 (1943): 370–96, https://psycnet.apa.org/doi/10.1037/h0054346.

7. Saul McLeod, "Maslow's Hierarchy of Needs," Simply Psychology, January 24, 2024, https://www.simplypsychology.org/maslow.html.

8. Alexandra Horowitz in *An Immense World: How Animal Senses Reveal the Hidden Realms Around Us*, Ed Yong (Random House Publishing Group, 2016), 13, Kindle.

9. Alexandra Horowitz in *An Immense World*, 22, Kindle.

10. Alexandra Horowitz in *An Immense World*, 18, Kindle.

11. Robin Wall Kimmerer, *Braiding Sweetgrass: Indigenous Wisdom, Scientific Knowledge, and the Teachings of Plants* (Milkweed Editions, 2013), 344.

12. Michael Schaffer, *One Nation Under Dog: Adventures in the New World of Prozac-Popping Puppies, Dog-Park Politics, and Organic Pet Food* (Holt, 2009), 39, Kindle.

13. Michael Schaffer, *One Nation Under Dog*, 39, Kindle.

## Chapter 13: Crafting Your Sacred Story: Communicating with Others

1. Pamela A. Hays, *Addressing Cultural Complexities in Practice: A Framework for Clinicians and Counselors* (American Psychological Association, 2007).

2. Lodro Rinzler, as quoted in Liza Kindred, *Eff This! Meditation: 108 Tips, Tricks, and Ideas for When You're Feeling Anxious, Stressed Out, or Overwhelmed* (Rock Point, 2019).

3. Janet Conner, *Writing Down Your Soul: How to Activate and Listen to the Extraordinary Voice Within* (Mango Media, 2021).

4. Janet Conner, *Writing Down Your Soul*, 7.

5. Janet Conner, *Writing Down Your Soul*, 7.

6. Janet Conner explores the science that supports the power of writing to help us gain new insights in a chapter titled "Why Write?" in *Writing Down Your Soul*.

# Selected Bibliography

Aftandilian, Dave, Barbara R. Ambros, and Aaron Gross, eds. *Animals and Religion*. Taylor & Francis, 2024.

Akers, Keith. Disciples: *How Jewish Christianity Shaped Jesus and Shattered the Church*. Apocryphile Press, 2013.

Ambros, Barbara. *Bones of Contention: Animals and Religion in Contemporary Japan*. University of Hawaii Press, 2012.

Ambros, Barbara. "Celebrating Creation and Commemorating Life: Ritualizing Pet Death in the U.S. and Japan." In *The Routledge History of Death Since 1800*, edited by Peter N. Stearns. Taylor & Francis, 2021.

Arluke, Arnold. *Just a Dog: Understanding Animal Cruelty and Ourselves*. Temple University Press, 2001.

Arluke, Arnold, and Clinton R. Sanders. *Regarding Animals*. Temple University Press, 2010.

Barker, Sandra B., and Randolph T. Barker. "The Human–Canine Bond: Closer Than Family Ties?" *Journal of Mental Health Counseling* 10, no. 1 (1988): 46–56. https://psycnet.apa.org/record/1989-01200-001.

Becker, Ernest. *The Denial of Death*. Free Press Paperbacks, 1973.

Bekoff, Marc. *The Emotional Lives of Animals: A Leading Scientist Explores Animal Joy, Sorrow, and Empathy—and Why They Matter*. New World Library, 2010.

Berry, Wendell. *The Unsettling of America: Culture and Agriculture*. Sierra Club Books, 1977.

Buber, Martin. *I and Thou*. Scribner, 1958.

Bussolari, Cori et al. "Self-Compassion, Social Constraints, and Psychosocial Outcomes in a Pet Bereavement Sample." *OMEGA Journal of Death and Dying* 82, no. 3 (2021): 389–408. http://dx.doi.org/10.1177/0030222818814050.

Challenger, Melanie. *How to Be Animal: A New History of What It Means to Be Human*. Penguin, 2021.

Charmaz, Kathy, and Melinda Milligan. "Grief." In *The Handbook of the Sociology of Emotions*, edited by Jan Stets and Jonathan H. Turner. Springer Science & Business Media, 2007.

Davis, Helen, et al. "When a Pet Dies: Religious Issues, Euthanasia and Strategies for Coping with Bereavement." *Anthrozoös* 16, no. 1 (2003). https://doi.org/10.2752/089279303786992378.

DeMello, Margo. *Animals and Society: An Introduction to Human-Animal Studies*. Columbia University Press, 2012.

de Waal, Frans. *Are We Smart Enough to Know How Smart Animals Are?* W. W. Norton & Company, 2019.

Doka, Kenneth. *Disenfranchised Grief: Recognizing Hidden Sorrow*. Lexington Books, 1989.

Grier, Katherine. *Pets in America: A History*. University of North Carolina Press, 2006.

Katz, John. *Soul of a Dog: Reflections on the Spirits of the Animals of Bedlam Farm*. Random House, 2009.

Kemmerer, Lisa. *Animals and Christianity*. Tapestry, 2022.

King, Barbara J. *Being with Animals: Why We Are Obsessed with the Furry, Scaly, Feathered Creatures Who Populate Our World*. Doubleday, 2010.

Knapp, Caroline. *Pack of Two: The Intricate Bond between People and Dogs*. Random House, 2010.

Kogan, Lori R., et al. "Pet Death and Owners' Memorialization Choices." *Illness, Crisis & Loss* 32, no. 2 (2022). https://doi.org/10.1177/10541373221143046.

Kogan, Lori R., et al. "Veterinary Technicians and Occupational Burnout." *Frontiers in Veterinary Science* 7 (2020). https://doi.org/10.3389/fvets.2020.00328.

Koudounaris, Paul. "The Rainbow Bridge: The True Story Behind History's Most Influential Piece of Animal Mourning Literature." The Order of the Good Death. February 9, 2023. https://www.orderofthegooddeath.com/article/the-rainbow-bridge-the-true-story-behind-historys-most-influential-piece-of-animal-mourning-literature/.

Kowalski, Gary. *Goodbye Friend: Healing Wisdom for Anyone Who Has Ever Lost a Pet*. New World Library, 1997.

Kowalski, Gary. *The Souls of Animals*. New World Library, 2001.

Liechty, Daniel J. *Transference and Transcendence: Ernest Becker's Contribution to Psychotherapy*. Jason Aronson Inc., 1995.

Linzey, Andrew, and Clair Linzey, eds. *Animal Theologians*. Oxford University Press, 2023.

Louv, Richard. *Our Wild Calling: How Connecting with Animals Can Transform Our Lives—and Save Theirs*. Algonquin Books, 2020.

McCutcheon, Kelly, and Stephen J. Fleming. "Grief Resulting from Euthanasia and Natural Death of Companion Animals." *Omega* 44, (2002): 169–188. https://doi.org/10.2190/5QG0-HVH8-JED0-ML16.

Merchant, Carolyn. *The Death of Nature: Women, Ecology, and the Scientific Revolution*, 2nd Edition. Harper Collins, 2019.

Morell, Virginia. *Animal Wise: How We Know Animals Think and Feel*. Broadway Books, 2013.

O'Donohue, John. *Anam Cara: A Book of Celtic Wisdom*. HarperCollins, 1997.

Park, Rachel, and Kenneth Royal. "A National Survey of Companion Animal Owners' Self-Reported Methods of Coping Following Euthanasia." *Veterinary Science* 7, no. 3 (2020): 89. https://doi.org/10.3390/vetsci7030089.

Pierce, Jessica. *Run Spot Run: The Ethics of Keeping Pets*. The University of Chicago Press, 2016.

Pierce, Jessica. *The Last Walk: Reflections on Our Pets at the End of Their Lives*. The University of Chicago Press, 2014.

Royal, Kenneth D., April A. Kedrowicz, and Amy M. Snyder. "Do All Dogs Go to Heaven? Investigating the Association between Demographic Characteristics and Beliefs about Animal Afterlife." *Anthrozoös* 29, no. 3 (2016): 409–420. https://doi.org/10.1080/08927936.2016.1189748.

Schaffer, Michael. *One Nation Under Dog: Adventures in the New World of Prozac-Popping Puppies, Dog-Park Politics, and Organic Pet Food*. Holt, 2009.

Scully, Matthew. *Dominion: The Power of Man, the Suffering of Animals, and the Call to Mercy*. St. Martin's Press, 2002.

Serpell, James. *In the Company of Animals: A Study of Human-Animal Relationships*, 2nd Edition. Cambridge University Press, 1996.

Singer, Peter, ed. *In Defense of Animals*. Blackwell Publishing, 2006.

Solomon, Sheldon, Jeff Greenberg, and Tom Pyszczynski. *The Worm at the Core: On the Role of Death in Life*. Random House, 2015.

Tuan, Yi-Fu. *Dominance and Affection: The Making of Pets*. Yale University Press, 1984.

Wall Kimmerer, Robin. *Braiding Sweetgrass: Indigenous Wisdom, Scientific Knowledge, and the Teachings of Plants*. Milkweed Editions, 2013.

Yong, Ed. *An Immense World: How Animal Senses Reveal the Hidden Realms Around Us*. Random House, 2022.

# Index